INSIGHT ◉ GUIDES

GERMANY

POCKET GUIDE

⊙ Walking Eye App

YOUR FREE EBOOK AVAILABLE THROUGH THE WALKING EYE APP

Your guide now includes a free eBook to your chosen destination,
for the same great price as before. Simply download the Walking Eye
App from the App Store or Google Play to access your free eBook.

HOW THE WALKING EYE APP WORKS

Through the Walking Eye App, you can purchase a range of eBooks and destination
content. However, when you buy this book, you can download the corresponding
eBook for free. Just see below in the grey panel where to find your free content and
then scan the QR code at the bottom of this page.

Destinations: Download essential destination content featuring recommended sights and attractions, restaurants, hotels and an A–Z of practical information, all available for purchase.

Ships: Interested in ship reviews? Find independent reviews of river and ocean ships in this section, all available for purchase.

eBooks: You can download your free accompanying digital version of this guide here. You will also find a whole range of other eBooks, all available for purchase.

Free access to travel-related blog articles about different destinations, updated on a daily basis.

HOW THE EBOOKS WORK

The eBooks are provided in EPUB file format. Please note that you will need an eBook reader installed on your device to open the file. Many devices come with this as standard, but you may still need to install one manually from Google Play.

The eBook content is identical to the content in the printed guide.

HOW TO DOWNLOAD THE WALKING EYE APP

1. Download the Walking Eye App from the App Store or Google Play.
2. Open the app and select the scanning function from the main menu.
3. Scan the QR code on this page – you will then be asked a security question to verify ownership of the book.
4. Once this has been verified, you will see your eBook in the purchased ebook section, where you will be able to download it.

Other destination apps and eBooks are available for purchase separately or are free with the purchase of the Insight Guide book.

914.304
Insight
2018

TOP 10 ATTRACTIONS

SCHLOSS NEUSCHWANSTEIN
Mad King Ludwig's fantastical castle is Germany's most popular visitor attraction. See page 117.

ROTHENBURG OB DER TAUBER
One of the most perfectly preserved medieval towns in Europe. See page 128.

THE RHINE VALLEY
At its most dramatic in the gorge near the town of Bacharach. See page 92.

SAXONY'S 'LITTLE SWITZERLAND'
Spectacular rock formations in the region south of Dresden. See page 63.

THE BRANDENBURG GATE
An enduring symbol of Berlin. See page 30.

THE DEUTSCHES MUSEUM IN MUNICH
A treasure house of science, technology and invention. See page 114.

MUNICH'S ALTE PINAKOTHEK
One of the world's great art galleries. See page 113.

THE KÖNIGSEE
Its pristine waters give views of the Watzmann, one of the highest peaks of the Bavarian Alps. See page 119.

COLOGNE CATHEDRAL
One of the greatest Gothic churches of Christendom. See page 84.

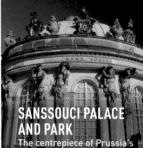

SANSSOUCI PALACE AND PARK
The centrepiece of Prussia's royal city, Potsdam. See page 42.

A PERFECT DAY

9.00am

Breakfast

A reservation at Käfer, the rooftop restaurant in the Reichstag, is a civilised way to avoid the long entry queues to go up to the glass dome.

2.00pm

River cruise

Head up to the Schiffbauerdamm boat landing (at Weidendammer Brücke) for a cruise along the River Spree. The shortest tours last around an hour and take in the new government quarter plus other Berlin highlights.

10.00am

Morning walk

Take a morning walk through the symbolic Brandenburg Gate and down Unter den Linden. Rub shoulders with Otto von Bismarck, Albert Einstein and Lady Gaga in Madame Tussauds at Unter den Linden 74.

12 noon

Retail therapy

Turn into Friedrichstrasse for a spot of shopping on Berlin's designer mile. Take a look at the huge multicoloured sculpture in the Quartier 205 building and stop for lunch in its excellent food court.

4.00pm

Café culture

Walk back to Unter den Linden to sample some rich German cakes at the old-worldly Operncafé. The pink baroque building opposite houses the fascinating German Historical Museum.

IN BERLIN

6.00pm

Sunset panorama
Take Europe's fastest lift up the red-brick Kohlhoff Tower at Potsdamer Platz for a perfect sunset view from the top-floor Panorama platform (closes 8pm). You get a similar view from the late-opening Solar bar and restaurant (Stresemannstrasse 76; cross the back yard to find the glass lift).

5.00pm

Big buildings
Explore the modern architecture at Potsdamer Platz (the 200 bus takes you right there from Unter den Linden) and stop at the ticket booth in the Arkaden mall if you fancy catching a performance by the Blue Man Group at 6 or 9pm.

9.00pm

On the town
Time to explore Berlin's nightlife. A good place to start is the Kulturbrauerei, a converted old brewery in Prenzlauer Berg with limitless other club and bar options within walking distance. The U2 underground line takes you there; get off at Eberswalder Strasse and walk down Schönhauser Allee to Sredzkistrasse.

7.00pm

Dinner time
Enjoy dinner at one of the area's many restaurants. Good options are Diekmann at the Weinhaus Huth, or the Sony Center across the street, where you can dine while marvelling at the spectacular architecture.

CONTENTS

INTRODUCTION

With 82.8 million inhabitants, the Federal Republic of Germany (*Bundesrepublik Deutschland*) is the most populous country in the European Union and one of the largest, covering an area of 357,000 sq km (138,000 sq miles). Some of its frontiers are formed by natural boundaries such as the North Sea and Baltic to the north, and the Alps to the south. In the north and west, the climate is maritime and temperate, moderated by the North Sea and the fading embers of the Gulf Stream. To the east, a continental weather pattern generally holds, characterised by hot summers and cold winters. The southern Alps have, almost by definition, an alpine climate, with altitude delivering cooler temperatures in summer and plenty of snow come winter.

TODAY'S GERMANY

Germany remains the economic powerhouse of Europe. Its industrial products are second to none, its towns and cities are linked by a superlative network of *Autobahnen* (motorways) and high-speed railway lines, and its people continue to enjoy one of the world's highest standards of living. The reunification of the country in 1990 was accomplished peacefully, and billions have been spent on bringing the infrastructure of former East Germany (GDR) up to Western standards. Nevertheless, differences in attitude continue to distinguish people from the East (*'Ossis'*) and West

State size

The largest of Germany's *Länder* is Bavaria (70,546 sq km/27,238 sq miles), the smallest the port-city states of Hamburg (755 sq km/292 sq miles) and Bremen (404 sq km/156 sq miles).

(['Wessis']). Unemployment is still a problem, particularly among young and elderly people in the east. The level had been coming down since record highs in 2005 until the global financial crisis hit in 2008, reversing some of the gains. With the country's emergence from recession in late 2009 and a continued growth in GDP and the all-important export sector through 2017, the trend in unemployment turned

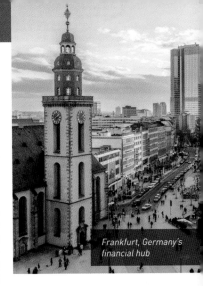

Frankfurt, Germany's financial hub

favourable once again. However, parts of the east are becoming depopulated as their inhabitants move away in search of work, and there are fears that a declining and ageing population will be unable to maintain the high standard of social welfare that Germans have become used to.

REGIONAL DIVERSITY

For most of its history, Germany was not a united country, but was divided into myriad states and a number of prosperous cities proudly maintained their independence. This has left an extraordinary array of capital cities.

Until 1871, Berlin was the capital of Prussia and, despite its subsequent growing importance as the national capital, other cities continued to think of themselves as the natural focus of their regions. This was especially true in post-war West Germany, with Berlin embedded deep behind the Iron Curtain.

Bavarian dancers in full swing

While the little Rhineland town of Bonn became the seat of the West German government, cities such as Cologne, Düsseldorf, Frankfurt, Hanover and Hamburg flourished, with Frankfurt, becoming the country's financial capital. Munich, seat of a monarch as recently as 1918, has never thought of itself as anything other than a capital city. The continuing importance of Germany's regions and regional capitals finds expression in the country's decentralised, federal political structure; its 16 states (*Land*, *Länder* plural) have many powers and responsibilities held by central government in other countries.

Most of Germany's cities suffered terrible devastation in World War II. In the West, they were swiftly rebuilt, with many historic buildings immaculately restored. In the East, funds and sometimes the will were lacking for a comparable effort, but since reunification much has been accomplished. In 2005 Dresden's completely rebuilt Frauenkirche (Church of Our Lady) was finally reconsecrated. In the former East Berlin, the vast Berliner Stadtschloss (Berlin City Palace) – the seat of imperial Germany's Kaisers, which was destroyed by World War II Allied bombing – is being rebuilt.

Outside the cities, the countryside has a wealth of castles, palaces, abbeys and, in the Catholic south, pilgrimage churches. There are also some of the most perfectly preserved small historic towns in Europe, including the succession of exquisite little cities like Rothenburg ob der Tauber strung out along the Romantic Road heading southwards to the Alps.

VARIED LANDSCAPES

The most spectacular peaks are those of the Bavarian Alps, but mountains and upland massifs cover much of the country, where there are endless opportunities for hiking. Lakes abound, the largest, Lake Constance, is a veritable inland sea shared with Austria and Switzerland. The upland massifs are threaded by rivers, the greatest of which is the Rhine, at its most scenic in the castle-studded gorge between Bingen and

⊘ ENVIRONMENTAL ISSUES

Recycling waste is almost a national obsession, and the environmental impact of new developments such as motorways arouses fierce passions and often determined opposition. From 1998 to 2005, the Green Party was the minority partner in a coalition government with the Social Democrats and was able to advance its environmental agenda, most notably with the decision to end nuclear power generation by 2022. The number of wind turbines, solar cells and biogas power stations has been steadily increasing to meet ambitious targets for renewable energy and reducing greenhouse gas emissions. However, coal production has increased, in part to offset the loss of nuclear power. In 2010, national controversy arose when the governing Conservative and Liberal coalition attempted to postpone the decommissioning of Germany's 17 nuclear power stations.

Koblenz. Other waterways are just as attractive, especially where their banks are graced with vineyards, like the Mosel, Main in the west, and the Elbe in the east.

The Germans love the beaches of the North Sea and Baltic, and the seaside is perhaps best enjoyed on one of the many islands, from Borkum, the westernmost of the Frisian islands, to Rügen in the Baltic, Germany's largest island.

GREEN GERMANY

Woodlands cover approximately a third of Germany's surface, a greatly appreciated background to everyday life and the inspiration for much art and literature. Spruce, fir and pine dominate mountains and heathlands, but the Germans' sacred tree, the stately oak, is suffering the effects of climate change, with one in every two oak trees officially sick.

ACTIVITIES

Germany has plenty of recreational facilities ranging from lavish theme parks to Olympic-sized swimming pools and well-signposted walking and cycling routes. Steamers ply Lake Constance and the major rivers while silent electric craft skim the pristine waters of the Königsee. Cable cars whisk sightseers to the tops of mountains, while, veteran steam trains chug along dozens of *Museumsbahnen* (preserved railway lines).

The majority of visitors come to Germany between May and September, when the weather is warm. July and August are the wettest months, though it is rare for rain to persist for more than a day or two. The big cities make excellent short-break destinations throughout the year. Winters bring cold, occasionally freezing weather, with fairly reliable snow cover in the Alps between December and March.

A BRIEF HISTORY

Even more than most great European countries, Germany has had a turbulent history. The nation had to wait until the late 19th century to achieve unity, only to lose it after defeat in World War II. Greeted initially with great joy, the reunification of 1990 has not been an unqualified success, and has reminded many Germans that most of their history has been a story of division and conflict as well as striking achievement in many spheres.

GERMANS AND ROMANS

In the final centuries BC, much of the area of present-day Germany was occupied by Celtic peoples. By the time the Roman Empire began its north-ward expansion in the 1st century BC, the Celts had moved away, escaping the pressure of Germanic tribes leaving their ancestral lands to the north and east. After their conquest of Celtic Gaul – today's France – the Romans turned east-wards, pushing the empire's frontier to the line of the Rhine and Danube. First contact with the Germans lurking in their vast forests inclined the Romans to dismiss them as indolent barbarians, given to

Hermann, conqueror of legions and the first Germanic hero

Frankish domains

The memory of the Franks is preserved in names like France (Frankreich in German), Frankfurt, where they forded the River Main, and the province of Franconia (Franken).

excessive eating and drinking. Attempts to bring them within the orbit of the empire included inviting prominent tribesmen to be educated in Rome and serve in the Roman army. This policy backfired when one German secretly roused his people to resist Roman expansion and, at the Battle of the Teutoburger Wald in AD9, annihilated three Roman legions by guiding them into a trap. This first Germanic hero was Hermann, whose resistance to Rome gave him cult-like status to German nationalists of a much later date. Following their defeat, the Romans prudently remained on the Rhine, giving the lands to the west of the river their usual treatment of ruler-straight roads, well-planned towns and luxurious villas. They also introduced Christianity and the cultivation of the vine.

CHARLEMAGNE

The collapse of the Roman Empire in the West in the 4th and 5th century AD was in part brought about by the restlessness of the Germanic tribes, who refused to be confined to their homelands. The most powerful group was the Franks, whose realm extended east and west of present-day Belgium.

Their greatest ruler was Charles the Great (Charlemagne in French, Karl der Grosse in German), who created a centralised feudal state. He deliberately associated himself with the glory and prestige of Roman rule, having himself crowned emperor by Pope Leo III in Rome in the year 800. Though his main base was at Aachen, Charles constantly moved around his dominions from one Imperial palace to the next, setting a pattern for later emperors and putting off the emergence of a geographical centre and capital city for Germany as a whole.

EMPERORS, PRINCES AND POPES

Later rulers of what came to be known as the 'Holy Roman Empire of the German Nation' failed to exercise the same measure of control as Charlemagne. Throughout the Middle Ages, nominally subordinate princes and other petty rulers contested the authority of the emperor, the focus of whose attention was frequently on his possessions in Italy and on his relations with the pope. From the Vatican, successive popes interfered in German affairs, asserting their supremacy as spiritual ruler over that of the emperor as temporal lord, and undermining him by encouraging his underlings to rebel. Though Germany thus

A pope and an emperor, Cologne Cathedral

Martin Luther

remained divided, there was much progress. Led by Lübeck, the Hanseatic League of trading cities promoted commerce along the shores of the Baltic and beyond; great cities like Nuremberg began their rise, and German settlers colonised much of Slavonic central and eastern Europe, founding towns and villages and bringing Christianity with them, sometimes at the point of the sword. In the middle of the 15th century, Johannes Gutenberg of Mainz ushered in a new era with his invention of moveable type, revolutionising book production.

REFORMATION AND WAR

Gutenberg's invention helped spread criticism of a Church that had become lazy and corrupt, and ensured that the teachings of reformer Martin Luther (1483–1546) reached a wide audience. Luther's ideas were taken up by many German rulers, one of whom, Friedrich III of Saxony, gave him sanctuary in Wartburg Castle. By the mid 16th century, Germany's division into a complex patchwork of Protestant and Catholic domains was complete, with Lutheranism dominating the north, Catholicism the south. Far from bringing stability, this arrangement led to the horrors of the Thirty Years' War (1618–48), in which German fought German, foreign powers like France and Sweden sought their own advantage, and mercenary soldiers plundered and pillaged at will. The war only came to an end with the total exhaustion of the combatants, leaving a devastated and depopulated landscape.

FRENCH DOMINANCE

In the aftermath of war, France became the leading power in Europe, and it was France that German rulers admired and sought to imitate. The Holy Roman Empire was a much diminished force. All over Germany, princes strove to turn their residences into a facsimile of Louis XIV's glittering court at Versailles. Palaces were extravagantly built or rebuilt in baroque style and provided with formal gardens on the French model, while in the court French was spoken, and the great prize was to have some French savant in residence, like Voltaire at Frederick the Great's Schloss Sanssouci at Potsdam. High culture flourished in this era, though not necessarily under the patronage of princes; at Leipzig, it was the city council that employed Johann Sebastian Bach (1685–1750) as town musician and choirmaster.

As the 18th century progressed, it became clear that Prussia was the coming power. Prussian monarchs ruled their realm on rational lines, promoting agriculture and industry, dispensing justice firmly but fairly, and creating a well-disciplined standing army capable of realising their territorial ambitions. But as the century ended, and the flames of the French Revolution spread all over Europe, no German power proved capable of stemming the conflagration.

NAPOLEON AND THE RISE OF NATIONALISM

For the first decade of the 19th century, it was a Frenchman, Napoleon Bonaparte, who determined the fate of Germany; he turned Bavaria, Württemberg and Saxony into kingdoms, amalgamated other German states into a subservient

Otto von Bismarck

'Confederation of the Rhine', and finally abolished the moribund Holy Roman Empire.

Napoleon's retreat from Moscow in 1812 unleashed passionate opposition to French domination as well as patriotic hopes for a new era of German unity and democracy. In 1813, Napoleon's army was bloodily defeated at Leipzig, at what came to be called the Battle of the Nations. But at the Congress of Vienna in 1815 the old order was restored, albeit tidied up, with dozens of minor German states abolished and absorbed into a new grouping of 39 sovereign units including a much-enlarged Prussia. For nearly 50 years, reactionary rulers succeeded in keeping the lid on progressive aspirations; an attempted revolution in 1848 petered out when the would-be revolutionaries argued interminably at their parliament in Frankfurt about the boundaries of a united Germany and how it should be ruled.

THE SECOND REICH

In the end, German unity was brought about not by upheaval from below or by reasoned discussion but by cynical diplomacy and armed force, under the leadership of an increasingly militaristic Prussia. A brief and victorious war with Austria in 1866 excluded the Habsburgs from German affairs, and left Prussia free to mould Germany as she wished. This she was able to do thanks to the skill and ruthlessness of her chancellor, Otto von Bismarck, who engineered another war, this time with France. Most of the other German states rallied to Prussia's side and victory was soon achieved. German unity was proclaimed in the Palace of Versailles in 1871, with Wilhelm I of Prussia as German emperor. Successor to the First Reich – the Holy Roman Empire – the Second Reich prospered and soon challenged the pre-eminence of Britain and France, particularly after the foolhardy and unstable Kaiser Wilhelm II succeeded to the throne in 1888.

WORLD WAR I

By the early 20th century Germany was a contradictory mixture: a great industrial power with a skilled and educated workforce, trade unions and advanced social legislation, but ruled by a monarch and court clad in medieval trappings and engaged in a game of international brinkmanship. When Austrian Archduke Franz Ferdinand was shot by a

☉ WEIMAR CULTURE

The Weimar years saw a flowering of cultural creativity. Literature and music flourished, and the sharpest of satirical cabarets enlivened the Berlin scene. German artists, designers and architects led the world, with the Bauhaus design school in Dessau becoming a byword for Modernist innovation. When the Nazis clamped down on such activity, the exiled professors and practitioners continued their work elsewhere, notably in the United States, where luminaries like Mies van der Rohe and Walter Gropius helped lay the foundations of a truly contemporary architecture.

Serb assassin at Sarajevo in June 1914, Germany recklessly encouraged Austria to declare war on Serbia. Europe's interlocking alliances were activated, with the 'central powers' of Austria and Germany facing Russia and France. Britain was drawn in when Germany violated Belgian neutrality, part of a long-prepared war plan to eliminate France quickly before turning on Russia. The plan failed when the German armies were stopped just short of Paris. Germany could not hope to win the war of attrition that followed, least of all when the United States entered the struggle in 1917, provoked by German submarine attacks on her shipping. By late 1918 defeat loomed and Wilhelm II went into ignominious exile in the Netherlands.

WEIMAR

In the chaotic situation following the armistice, the new government fled from revolutionary disturbances in Berlin to the safety of the small provincial town of Weimar. The little city gave its name to the democratic republic which somehow survived multiple misfortunes: the loss of territory to France and Poland, onerous reparation payments to the Allies, attempts to topple it from Right and Left, a French occupation of the Ruhr industrial area, and catastrophic inflation which destroyed the savings of the middle classes. By the late 1920s a degree of prosperity had returned, but by 1929 the Great Depression intervened. By 1932 German industry had collapsed, there were six million unemployed, and Nazis and Communists were confidently offering rival totalitarian solutions to the country's problems, as well as brawling with each other for control of the streets. Fearing a Red Revolution, in January 1933 the German establishment appointed Nazi Party leader Adolf Hitler as chancellor.

THE THIRD REICH

Hitler moved swiftly to consolidate his power, using the burning-down of the Reichstag in February 1933 as a pretext for imprisoning and intimidating his opponents and subsequently ruling by decree. The Nazis brought latent anti-Semitism into play, with the Jews made the scapegoat for all Germany's ills and forced into ever more constricting circumstances. Those who realised what was coming emigrated, along with a sizeable proportion of the country's cultural elite. Popular enthusiasm was maintained by means of stunning spectacles such as the Berlin Olympics of 1936 and the annual Nuremberg rallies. The young were conscripted into the Hitler Youth and turned into the regime's most fanatical supporters.

WORLD WAR II

Despite widespread support for the Nazi regime, many Germans were dismayed when war broke out in September 1939. A series of swift victories won by *Blitzkrieg* tactics over Poland, Norway, the Low Countries and France followed. However, the failure to eliminate Britain in the summer of 1940, the attack on the Soviet Union in June 1941 and the entry of the US into

Nazi parade under the Brandenburg Gate

the war in December of that year faced Germany with a coalition whose overwhelming superiority in resources meant that they must ultimately prevail. But Hitler could only conceive of death and destruction, and many of his minions in the SS were more interested in implementing the Final Solution – the murder of Europe's Jews – than winning the war. Two events sealed Germany's fate: the 1943 defeat at Stalingrad in the east, and the 1944 Normandy invasion in the west. In July 1944, an attempted assassination of Hitler by a group of army officers failed. The war went on for almost another year, causing more carnage and destruction than in the previous five put together. By April 1945 Hitler was dead, Germany's cities had been bombed into ruins, and millions of Germans had abandoned their homelands in the east for fear of a vengeful Red Army.

GERMANY DIVIDED

The victorious Allied forces now occupied Germany. After a short period of uneasy post-war cooperation between the western powers and the Soviets, each side created rival Germanys in its own image. In the west, the Bundesrepublik Deutschland, or Federal Republic of Germany, had a liberal democratic constitution and a burgeoning

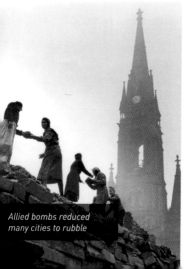

Allied bombs reduced many cities to rubble

economy. In the east was the Deutsche Demokratische Republik (DDR), or German Democratic Republic (GDR), a 'people's democracy' run on the lines of the Soviet Union's other satellites in Eastern Europe, and lagging well behind the West in economic achievement. Embedded in the GDR was Berlin, likewise divided into an eastern and western sector, the latter only having survived a year-long Soviet blockade in 1948–9 thanks to the near-miracle of the Berlin Airlift, in which US and British planes flew in every necessity of life, including bulk loads such as coal.

West Berlin proved a thorn in the GDR's side, allowing its dissatisfied citizens easy escape to the West. By 1961, some three million had left, and the collapse of the economy was only averted by building the Berlin Wall to keep the population in. Over the next three decades the GDR portrayed itself as one of the success stories of Communism. Statistics were manipulated to show that it was one of the world's leading industrial powers, with a welfare system that cared for its citizens from cradle to grave. In reality, the goods being produced were only saleable in Eastern Europe, polluting industries were destroying the environment, and social welfare existed alongside the *Stasi*, a secret police apparatus of almost unimaginable scope and complexity. By the late 1980s, the system was foundering; in 1989 popular discontent manifested itself in huge street demonstrations, and the regime's collapse became inevitable when Mikhail Gorbachev's Soviet Union withdrew its support.

DIE WENDE

Meaning 'the turning point', 'die Wende' is the German term for the momentous changes that took place following the collapse of the Berlin Wall on 9 November 1989. For a while, it

Angela Merkel

seemed possible that an East German state of some kind might continue to exist, even after the Communist regime had realised that the game was up and had handed over power to an interim government. Many felt that the differences between the two German states were so profound that a period of transition would be needed before any decision about reunification could be taken. But the West German Chancellor, Helmut Kohl, had no such doubts; greeted by enthusiastic crowds on his tours of the East, he declared 'My goal... is the unity of the nation!'

This unity was achieved on 3 October 1990, by a straightforward absorption of the GDR into the Bundesrepublik rather than a confederation of the two states. Chancellor Kohl promised the Bundesrepublik's new citizens 'blossoming landscapes', but despite huge investment in the East this shared prosperity and wellbeing has taken far longer to achieve than Kohl and his listeners ever imagined. In 1998 Kohl's Christian Democrats were defeated in the general election. In 2005, with a new, charismatic female leader Angela Merkel, they managed to regain power; yet since 2013 they have had to govern the country together with their traditional rivals, the Social Democrats, forming the so-called Grand Coalition (Große Koalition).

HISTORICAL LANDMARKS

5th–1st century BC Germany inhabited by Celts.

58BC Julius Caesar halts westwards move by Germanic tribes.

AD9 Romans defeated at the Battle of the Teutoburger Wald.

4th–5th centuries Collapse of the Roman Empire; westwards migration of Germanic peoples.

800 Frankish ruler Charlemagne crowned Emperor of the West.

1241 Foundation of Hanseatic League of ports and trading cities.

1386 Foundation of the first German university, at Heidelberg.

1517 Martin Luther nails his 95 theses to the church door at Wittenberg, marking the start of the Reformation.

1618–48 Thirty Years' War devastates and depopulates Central Europe.

1701 Rise of Prussia begins with crowning of Elector Friedrich III as king.

1806 Napoleon dominates Germany with the creation of the Confederation of the Rhine and the abolition of the Holy Roman Empire.

1813 Napoleon's defeat at the 'Battle of the Nations'.

1815 Congress of Vienna disappoints hopes for German unity.

1871 Prussian King Wilhelm proclaimed emperor of united Germany.

1914–18 World War I ends in defeat of Germany.

1933 Nazi Party leader Adolf Hitler appointed Reich chancellor.

1945 Defeat of Nazi Germany ends World War II in Europe.

1949 Division into western Federal Republic and eastern Communist-led German Democratic Republic.

1961 Berlin Wall built to stem the number of GDR citizens escaping to West Germany.

1989 Berlin Wall demolished; collapse of Communist regime.

1990 GDR absorbed into the Federal Republic; Germany reunited.

2005 Angela Merkel becomes Germany's first female chancellor.

2014 Germany wins the football World Cup in Brazil.

2016 Berlin attack: Tunisian migrant hijacks a lorry and runs it into a crowded Christmas market, killing 12.

2018 Angela Merkel, elected for the fourth time, forms a new coalition government of the CDU, CSU and SPD.

Potsdamer Platz

WHERE TO GO

BERLIN AND POTSDAM

Germany's federal capital, **Berlin** ❶ is one of the most dynamic and exciting cities of Europe, attracting visitors from around the globe. The city's most visual symbol, the Brandenburger Tor (Brandenburg Gate), stands at its heart, rather than marking the division between East and West as it did more than two decades ago.

Nearby, the Reichstag houses the nation's parliament, and in the Mitte district, the historic city centre, museums, galleries, theatres and other monuments form one of the world's great cultural ensembles. The Friedrichstrasse artery is lined with prestigious retail palaces and glittering shopping arcades, their equivalents in western Berlin being the well-established stores lining the Kurfürstendamm boulevard. Many of the vast redevelopment projects, like the one at Potsdamer Platz, have been completed, and smaller projects continue to change the cityscape. Inner-city boroughs like fast gentrifying Prenzlauer Berg have been blossoming, while Kreuzberg remains the stronghold of alternative lifestyles and of Berlin's Turkish population. To the west, affluent suburban boroughs like Wilmersdorf and Zehlendorf benefit from their proximity to the vast Grunewald forest and the chain of lakes along the River Havel, while in the south the former Tempelhof Airport has been turned into the city's biggest public park. Potsdam, a regal little city just to the west of Berlin and capital of the Land of Brandenburg, is a place where princes, kings and emperors built their palaces in a quiet countryside of sandy soils, pine forests and slow-moving rivers.

BRANDENBURG GATE AREA

Marking the western boundary of the city when it was built in 1791, the **Brandenburger Tor** Ⓐ is Berlin's last remaining gateway. The scene of many a military parade in past times, the gate is now best remembered as the backdrop to the ecstatic scenes which took place following the fall of the Berlin Wall. The famous Quadriga, a statue of Victory driving her four-horse chariot, is a replica, the original having been destroyed in World War II.

To the east and west stretch broad, straight thoroughfares. Leading to Museum Island, the boulevard **Unter den Linden** ('Beneath the Lime Trees') was laid out by Prussian rulers as their most prestigious street and lined with dignified neoclassical buildings. Facing each other are the State Opera and Humboldt University, while in the grid of streets to the south is **Gendarmenmarkt**, a glorious architectural ensemble of buildings including French and German cathedrals.

On the far side of the Brandenburger Tor, the Strasse des 17 Juni (17 June Street) penetrates the **Tiergarten**, the vast and splendid parkland which was once a royal hunting preserve. The Tiergarten is a wonderful asset to have in the centre of a metropolis, though its trees are almost all relatively recent plantings, most of their predecessors having been felled for fuel in the difficult post-war period.

To the north is the government quarter, its cool, modern buildings spanning the River Spree and symbolically breaking down the old boundary between East and West Berlin. One focal

Greek inspiration

The design of the Brandenburg Gate was inspired by the Propylea, the grand entrance to the Acropolis in Athens, and was originally called the Friedenstor (Gate of Peace).

Brandenburger Tor

point here is the box-like Kanzleramt, the office of the federal chancellor, but anchoring today's government to the country's past is the massive **Reichstag** Ⓑ (www.bundestag.de; 8am–midnight, last admission 9.45pm; free). Completed in 1894, in 1933 the Reichstag was gutted by a fire almost certainly started by the Nazis, and further devastated by the fierce fighting of 1945. Since 1999 it has once more been the seat of parliament (Bundestag), its exterior lightened by the superb glass and steel cupola placed atop it by the British architect Sir Norman Foster and illuminating the debating chamber with natural light.

MUSEUM ISLAND

Enclosed between two arms of the River Spree, Berlin's **Museumsinsel** Ⓒ (Museum Island; www.museumsinsel-berlin.de) formed part of the original, 13th-century core of the city. It owes its name to the cluster of world-class museums which contain some of the country's finest collections. The island is reached from Unter den Linden via the elegant **Schlossbrücke** (Palace Bridge), designed by the great Prussian architect Karl Friedrich Schinkel in 1824. On the northern side of the approach to the bridge is the baroque **Zeughaus** (Arsenal) – the home of the **Deutsches Historisches Museum** (German Historical Museum; www.dhm.de; daily 10am–6pm) – and, next door, the **Neue Wache** (New Guardhouse), a perfectly proportioned little neo-Grecian temple by Schinkel now dedicated to the victims of war and tyranny.

Beyond the bridge is Schinkel's masterpiece, the neoclassical **Altes Museum** (Old Museum; www.smb.museum; Tue–Sun 10am–6pm, Thu until 8pm), its long colonnaded facade overlooking the grassy expanse of the Lustgarten. It houses an outstanding collection of classical antiquities.

To its rear is the **Alte Nationalgalerie** (Old National Gallery; www.smb.museum; Tue–Sun 10am–6pm, Thu until 8pm), which houses an excellent collection of 19th-century German art. The **Neues Museum** (New Museum; www.smb.museum; daily 10am–6pm, Thu until 8pm) houses pre- and early history collections, including superlative items from ancient Egypt such as the famous bust of Nefertiti.

The most grandiose of the island's museums is the **Pergamonmuseum** (www.smb.museum; daily 10am–6pm, Thu until 8pm), named after its most prized possession, the gigantic marble altar from the Hellenistic city of Pergamon. But this is just one of countless treasures from the world of classical antiquity, the Middle East and the Orient; make sure you see the great gateway from Miletus and the famous Ishtar Gate from Babylon. At the very tip of Museum Island, the **Bode-Museum** (www.smb.museum; Tue–Sun 10am–6pm, Thu until 10pm) is the permanent home for a range of collections including Byzantine art and the half-million items of the world-famous Münzkabinett (coin collection).

The Lustgarten is dominated by the formidable bulk of the **Berliner Dom** (Berlin Cathedral; www.berliner-dom.de; open daily but times vary), the cathedral completed in 1905 as the court church of the Hohenzollern royal family. Its bombastic architecture perfectly evokes the spirit of Kaiser Wilhelm II's time.

Berliner Dom on the river

CHECKPOINT CHARLIE

Towards the southern end of Friedrichstrasse, the most notorious crossing-point between East and West, **Checkpoint Charlie**, has become one of Berlin's most popular sights. It was here, shortly after the building of the Berlin Wall in 1961, that US and Soviet tanks faced each other in one of the most tense stand-offs of the Cold War. Visitors are invited to pose with menacing-looking members of the People's Police or take a trip in a Trabant, the once-ubiquitous East German 'people's car'. But perhaps more rewarding is the **Museum Haus am Checkpoint Charlie – Mauermuseum** Ⓓ (Checkpoint Charlie Building Museum – Berlin Wall Museum; www.mauermuseum.de; daily 9am–10pm), whose displays feature the attempts made by East Germans to overcome the barrier of the Berlin Wall. Home-made aircraft and submarines were among the often ingenious means of escape.

ALEXANDERPLATZ AND AROUND

The draughty expanses on either side of the elevated Alexanderplatz railway station were the showcase of East Berlin in Communist times. Soaring over it all is the 365m (1,198ft) **Fernsehturm E** (TV Tower; www.tv-turm.de; viewing gallery daily Mar–Oct 9am–midnight, Nov–Feb 10am–midnight), deliberately designed to upstage West Berlin's far more modest Funkturm (Radio Tower). The panorama from the top takes in the whole of the city, and there is a revolving restaurant. Among

⊘ REMEMBERING HITLER'S VICTIMS

Berlin, which had harboured an exceptionally large and vibrant Jewish community, will never be forgotten as the place from which the extermination of European Jewry was planned and directed. The **Denkmal für die Ermordeten Juden Europas** (Memorial to the Murdered Jews of Europe; www.stiftung-denkmal.de; information centre: Apr–Sept Tue–Sun 10am–8pm (last admission 7.15pm), Oct–Mar Tue–Sun 10am–7pm (last admission 6.15pm); field open permanently; free) spreads over an extensive area to the south of the Brandenburg Gate. It consists of a vast and enigmatic field of 2,711 concrete slabs.

American, Polish-born Daniel Libeskind, was responsible for what has become one of Berlin's most visited museums, the **Jüdisches Museum** (Jewish Museum; www.juedisches-museum-berlin.de; daily 10am–8pm, last admission 7pm), its jagged outline and disorientating interior evocative of the troubled course of German-Jewish history.

Rotes Rathaus and Fernsehturm

the few remaining historic structures at the foot of the tower are the 13th-century **Marienkirche** (www.marienkirche-berlin.de) and the 19th-century **Rotes Rathaus** (Red Town Hall). Beyond the railway overpass, the high-rise slab of the Park Inn (formerly the 'Stadt Berlin', the GDR's foremost hotel) looks down on the rather tacky Weltzeituhr (World Time Clock) and the Brunnen der Völkerfreundschaft (Fountain of Friendship between the Peoples). Leading eastwards is the broad boulevard of Karl-Marx-Allee, laid out in the 1950s and known at the time as Stalin-Allee. The Soviet-inspired architecture of the apartment buildings lining it is now appreciated as a historic style in its own right.

More obviously appealing is the architecture of the **Nikolaiviertel** (Nicholas Quarter) to the south of the Rotes Rathaus. Centred on the twin-steepled Nikolaikirche, this little neighbourhood was completely rebuilt in near-authentic historic style as part of the city's 750th anniversary celebrations in 1987, and its intimate atmosphere, cafés, restaurants and shops have proved a great hit with visitors to the city.

Equally popular but with a different atmosphere altogether is the thriving area around **Hackescher Markt**, one S-Bahn stop west of Alexanderplatz. Very run-down in GDR times, this district is now buzzing with bars, cafés, clubs, galleries, art workshops, antiques dealers and independent shops. The area's centrepiece is the immaculately restored **Hackesche Höfe F**, an Art Deco complex of interconnecting courtyards and buildings. Oranienburger Strasse leads from here to one of the great monuments of Jewish Berlin, the **Synagoge** (New Synagogue; www.centrumjudaicum.de; Mar–Oct Sun–Mon 10am–8pm, Tue–Thu 10am–6pm, Fri 10am–5pm or until 2pm Mar and Oct, Nov–Feb Sun–Thu 10am–6pm, Fri 10am–2pm), its gleaming cupola visible from far away.

KURFÜRSTENDAMM AND AROUND

One of the great landmarks of West Berlin is the ruined **Kaiser-Wilhelm-Gedächtnis-Kirche G** (Kaiser Wilhelm Memorial Church; www.gedaechtniskirche.com; daily 9am–7pm), its bomb-blasted tower preserved as an instantly recognisable landmark. Flanked by a modern church and bell tower, it stands on Breitscheidplatz, a favourite meeting place.

⊘ BERLIN SIGHTSEEING BUSES

Soon after the reunification, two new bus lines were introduced to bring together the transport networks of East and West Berlin. Bus No. 100 crosses the city centre (Mitte), passing near virtually all major points of interest there, while No. 200 goes further east, terminating at Prenzlauer Berg. You can buy a regular Berlin transport ticket (for zones A and B), then use these buses for an inexpensive sightseeing tour of central Berlin.

Convenient starting points for a tour include the Zoological Garden (Zoologischer Garten) in the west or Alexanderplatz in the east. You can get off and on the buses as many times as you like within the two-hour timeframe of your ticket.

To the north is the **Zoological Garden** (www.zoo-berlin.de; daily 9am–6pm, with seasonal variations), which has one of the richest and most varied animal collections in Europe.

To the southeast, along Tauentzienstrasse, stands one of the world's great department stores, KaDeWe (Kaufhaus des Westens), a tourist attraction in its own right, not least because of its lavish sixth-floor delicatessen.

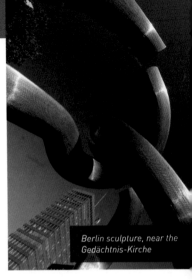

Berlin sculpture, near the Gedächtnis-Kirche

Further tempting retail opportunities multiply as you head west along Berlin's great shopping artery, **Kurfürstendamm** 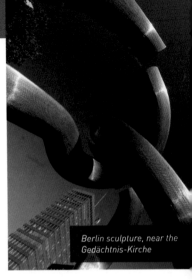, known simply as Ku'damm. Perhaps less glamorous now than in its 1950s and '60s heyday, its broad pavements still invite you to stroll and window-shop. There are more fascinating shops, boutiques, cafés and restaurants in the streets and squares to the north, particularly around **Savignyplatz**. Before leaving Ku'damm you might like to visit **The Story of Berlin** (www.story-of-berlin.de; daily 10am–8pm, last admission 6pm), which has excellent interactive multimedia displays tracing the city's turbulent past.

KULTURFORUM AND POTSDAMER PLATZ

Developed by West Berlin at a time when the city's division seemed permanent, the **Kulturforum** cultural complex rivals Museum Island in quality, though its collections are of a very different nature. The first building on the site, in 1963, was the tent-like structure of the **Philharmonie ❶**, designed by Hans Scharoun, its form perfectly reflecting its function as a superlative concert hall. Scharoun also designed the adjoining **Musikinstrumenten-Museum** (Museum of Musical Instruments; www.mim-berlin.de; Tue–Fri 9am–5pm, Thu until 8pm, Sat–Sun 10am–5pm), which has a fine collection of historic instruments, among them a Stradivarius violin of 1703 and an Art Deco Wurlitzer organ.

On the far side of the street, a sprawling structure houses several galleries. Foremost among them is the **Gemäldegalerie** (Picture Gallery; www.smb.museum; Tue–Sun 10am–6pm, Thu until 8pm), home of some of the world's finest paintings. Works by virtually all the great names in European art from the 13th to the 18th century can be found here; German Old Masters like Dürer and Cranach are particularly strongly represented and the Rembrandt collection is exceptional.

Also in this part of the Kulturforum are two smaller museums. The **Kupferstichkabinett** (Museum of Prints and Drawings; www.smb.museum; Tue–Fri 10am–6pm, Sat–Sun 11am–6pm) encompasses graphic art from the Middle Ages to the present. The **Kunstgewerbemuseum** (Museum of Decorative Arts; www.smb.museum; Tue–Fri 10am–6pm, Sat–Sun 11am–6pm) has a magnificent collection of European arts and crafts and interior design, from medieval and Renaissance handmade treasures to examples of contemporary industrial output.

Standing out among the late 20th-century buildings of the Kulturforum is the delicately detailed 19th-century neo-Romanesque brick church of **St Matthäuskirche**. It contrasts strikingly with the uncompromisingly modern **Neue Nationalgalerie** (New National Gallery; www.smb.museum; closed for renovation until 2020), a steel and glass building by Mies van der Rohe. As well as staging changing exhibitions of contemporary art, the gallery houses one of the country's

The Neue Nationalgalerie

finest collections of works by 20th-century German artists and their international counterparts.

On the far bank of the **Landwehrkanal** (Landwehr Canal) is the extensive and fascinating **Deutsches Technikmuseum** (German Technology Museum; www.dtmb.de; Tue–Fri 9am–5.30pm, Sat–Sun 10am–6pm). Poised above its entrance is a DC3 aircraft that took part in the Berlin Airlift. Inside, full-size exhibits and interactive displays deal with every aspect of technology, from trains to textiles.

To the east of the Kulturforum, the entertainment, shopping and business centre of **Potsdamer Platz** has become one of the great symbols of post-unification Berlin. Striking contemporary structures in and around the square include the **Sony Center**, whose stunning transparent dome shelters a spacious piazza. Here too is the **Deutsche Kinemathek** (German Cinematheque; www.deutsche-kinemathek.de; Tue–Sun

10am–6pm, Thu until 8pm), which celebrates the glory days of Berlin as Germany's Hollywood and includes a great deal of Marlene Dietrich memorabilia.

CHARLOTTENBURG AND FAR WESTERN BERLIN

One of the best places to experience the atmosphere of Prussian Berlin is the glorious rococo and baroque palace of **Schloss Charlottenburg** (www.spsg.de; Tue–Sun 10am–4.30pm, Apr–Oct until 5.30pm). Painstakingly restored after wartime damage, the interiors are of great sumptuousness, and are complemented by the park bounded by the winding River Spree. Further to the west stands the **Olympiastadion** (Olympic Stadium; www.olympiastadion-berlin.de; daily mid-Mar to Oct 9am–7pm (Jun to mid-Sept until 8pm), Nov to mid-Mar 10am–4pm; may be closed for events), its huge scale and mock classical architecture redolent of the Third Reich; it was built for the 1936 Nazi Olympics and refurbished for the 2006 football World Cup.

⊘ BERLINER SCHNAUZE

Like big-city folk in most countries, Berliners are renowned for their sharp wit and an unforgiving view of the world and its ways, sometimes described as *Berliner Schnauze* (Berlin lip). Pretentiousness is quickly deflated, notably in the nicknames given to certain features of the city. Thus the gaunt ruin of the Kaiser-Wilhelm Memorial Church became the 'Hollow Tooth', the bulbous Congress Hall the 'Pregnant Oyster', and the East Berlin TV Tower the 'Pope's Revenge' because of the big cross formed on its reflective surface by the sun. More recently, the federal chancellor's office, a big white boxy structure, has become known as the 'washing machine'.

The Dahlem district is home to the **Museen Dahlem**, another of the city's museum complexes. There are lavishly stocked museums of East Asian art and Indian art and others dealing with ethnography and European folk art (www.smb.museum; all museums Tue–Fri 10am–5pm, Sat–Sun 11am–6pm).

To the west of Dahlem and the other leafy suburbs extends the **Grunewald** forest, vast enough to get lost in and still the haunt of wild boar.

Schloss Charlottenburg

Beyond the trees, the glorious waters of the Wannsee, a linked pair of lakes on the River Havel, form one of Berlin's favourite recreation spots, its beaches crowded with swimmers and sun-worshippers in warm weather. There's a foretaste here of the splendours of royal Potsdam, with palaces and parklands on **Pfaueninsel** (Peacock Island) and at **Klein-Glienicke**. A temple at Klein-Glienicke overlooks the **Glienicker Brücke** (Glienicke bridge), famous as the East–West crossing point where Cold War rivals occasionally swapped spies in a tense atmosphere of mutual suspicion.

POTSDAM

The capital of the *Land* of Brandenburg, **Potsdam ❷**, about 30km (19 miles) southwest of the capital, is to Berlin what Versailles is to Paris, a royal residential town set among woods and lakeland, embellished with fine architecture and lovely man-made landscapes. Most of the rulers of Prussia left their mark here, most notably Frederick the Great, builder of Potsdam's outstanding palace, Sanssouci.

The centre of the little city was devastated in an Allied air raid in the final days of World War II, and suffered further neglect and demolition under the Communist regime. But there's still plenty to see, from the massive early 19th-century domed **Nikolaikirche** (Church of St Nicholas) to the gracious streets and villa quarters once occupied by Prussian officials and the officers of the city's important garrison. The charming, brick-built **Holländisches Viertel** (Dutch Quarter), laid out in the mid-18th century for immigrants from the Netherlands, now acts as a magnet for locals and visitors alike, with an inviting range of bars, restaurants and boutiques.

Beyond Potsdam's own **Brandenburger Tor** (Brandenburg Gate) at the western end of the town centre stretches the parkland of **Schloss Sanssouci** (www.spsg.de; Apr–Oct Tue–Sun 10am–5.30pm, Nov–Mar Tue–Sun 10am–4.30pm). The park is the leafy framework for an array of statuary, fountains, temples, residences and pavilions, the most exquisite of which is the **Chinesisches Teehaus** (Chinese Teahouse; May–Oct Tue–Sun 10am–5.30pm), which contains a collection of fine porcelain. And then there are the palaces. A flight of terraces intended for the cultivation of fruit and vines leads to the palace of Sanssouci, which was designed by Frederick the Great's architect Georg Wenzeslaus von

Potsdam Conference

In 1945, Schloss Cecilienhof was the venue for a meeting at which the Allied heads of government – Stalin, Churchill and Truman – settled the division of Europe after World War II.

Schloss Sanssouci

Knobelsdorff and completed in 1747. Its elegant interiors were the scene of much music-making, philosophising and high-minded conversation, for Frederick prided himself on his culture, even managing to attract French philosopher Voltaire to be an ornament of his court. At the far end of the park stands a very different sort of palace, the **Neues Palais** (New Palace), also built by Frederick but of overpowering size and ostentation.

In complete contrast, on the other side of the city is **Schloss Cecilienhof** (www.spsg.de; Apr–Oct Tue–Sun 10am–5.30pm, Nov–Mar until 4.30pm), an imitation Tudor country house only completed during World War I for Kaiser Wilhelm's son, the crown prince. It is now a luxury hotel.

SPREEWALD
Between Berlin and the border town of Cottbus, the River Spree spreads out into an inland delta, its countless channels shaded

Hamburg and its waterfront

by overhanging trees. This is the tranquil Spreewald, one of the homelands of the Sorbs, a Slav minority, whose ancestors managed to resist Germanisation. There's an open-air museum of their traditional buildings at **Lehde** (www.museum-osl.de; daily Apr–Oct 10.30am–5.30pm, Nov–Mar 1–4pm), close to the area's little capital of **Lübbenau**. Movement in this trackless wilderness was traditionally by punt, craft still used to ferry the visitors around who come to escape the pressures of the city. But it's easy to avoid the crowds, by walking, cycling or taking to the water in a hired canoe.

HAMBURG AND THE NORTH

Between the Dutch, Danish and Polish borders are some of Germany's most fascinating cities, many of them at the point where great rivers flow into the North Sea or the Baltic.

Foremost among them are the city states of Hamburg and Bremen, followed closely by other harbour towns which were once members of the Hanseatic League, the powerful trading association, and which have preserved much of their heritage.

The coast itself is almost infinitely varied, with islands, glorious sandy beaches, rich wildlife, dune systems, steep bluffs, wooded tracts and chalk cliffs. Busy seaside towns alternate with tranquil islands where traffic is banned, while the Baltic shore is graced by resorts little changed since their heyday a century ago. Inland is the extensive Mecklenburgische Seenplatte (Mecklenburg lake district), with its many lakes and deep forests.

HAMBURG

More than 100km (60 miles) upstream from the mouth of the mighty River Elbe, Germany's second city is its largest sea port and an important manufacturing centre. It's also a place of great contrasts: it boasts more millionaires than anywhere else in the country, but unemployment is high, and its generally sober ethos sits awkwardly with the raucous lifestyle epitomised by the city's red-light district, the Reeperbahn.

Hamburg ➌ began life as Hammaburg, a 9th-century fortress built by Charlemagne at the confluence of the little River Alster and the Elbe. For centuries the city lived in the shadow of Lübeck, the leader of the Hanseatic League, but once trading patterns had shifted from the Baltic to the wider world of the Atlantic,

Hamburg by boat

Less dramatic than a harbour tour, a pleasure-boat trip on the broader waters of the Aussenalster is nevertheless highly recommended, revealing something of the elegant inner suburban areas, home to the city's wealthier inhabitants.

Speicherstadt warehouses

Hamburg never looked back. This despite having to rebuild itself from scratch twice, once after a terrible blaze in 1842, and again after the devastating firestorm unleashed 101 years later by British air force bombers. Created a Free Imperial city in 1618, Hamburg considers itself a cut above the rest of Germany, a status confirmed by its continued existence as a *Land* in its own right. Its cultural life and its heritage of museums are the equal of many a capital city.

The Harbour and Beyond

A stroll along the waterfront is an excellent way of beginning to absorb the atmosphere of this great city and understand the reasons for its existence. The **Landungsbrücken** are the pontoons at which ocean liners used to tie up; this trade has gone, but there's still plenty of activity on the broad waters of the Elbe, as smaller craft mingle with the huge container ships making their way to and from the docks opposite. A cruise around the harbour in one of the many pleasure boats is an experience not to be missed, not least because of the views of Hamburg's distinctive skyline, dominated by the towers of the city's great churches. The highest at 132m (433ft) is that of the **St Michaelis-Kirche**, well worth the climb. Moored just to the east of the Landungsbrücken is the East India windjammer *Rickmer*

Rickmers, a splendid reminder of the great days of sail (daily 10am–6pm). Further east still is the extraordinary conglomeration of 19th-century multistorey red-brick warehouses known as the **Speicherstadt**, while 'inland' are the *Fleeten*, the canals lined with merchants' dwellings which formed Hamburg's first harbour. The **Nikolaifleet** is the best preserved of them, while the Alsterfleet threads through the Altstadt (old town) into the **Binnenalster**, the smaller of the city's two lovely lakes. It passes close to the **Rathaus**, the monumental city hall built in 1897 in Northern Renaissance style, a striking symbol of Hamburg's confidence, pride and prosperity. Contemporary prosperity is much in evidence in the **Alsterarkaden** overlooking the Alsterfleet and in the other arcades and streets to the north.

Museums

Several of Hamburg's museums are grouped along the broad semi-circular thoroughfare laid out along the line of the old city walls, in particular along its eastern section, known as the **Museumsmeile** (Museum Mile). The **Museum für Kunst und Gewerbe** (Decorative Arts Museum; www.mkg-hamburg.de; Tue–Sun 10am–6pm, Thu until 9pm) is one of the finest and most comprehensive of its kind in Germany, with superlative exhibits ranging from medieval reliquaries to complete Art Nouveau interiors; there's also an exceptional collection of antique keyboard instruments. The **Hamburger Kunsthalle** (Hamburg Art Gallery; www.hamburger-kunsthalle.de; Tue–Sun 10am–6pm, Thu until 9pm) ranks among the country's leading galleries. Its collection ranges from medieval times to the present, with contemporary works housed in a spacious extension. In the parkland at the western end of the old city walls stands the **Hamburgmuseum** (www.hamburgmuseum.de; Tue–Sat 10am–5pm, Sun 10am–6pm), expertly evoking every aspect of Hamburg's past. The vast

Lübeck's Holstentor

model railway, based on one of the city's principal stations, amazes young and old alike.

St Pauli and the Reeperbahn

A rather different institution has an appropriate location in the heart of the St Pauli red-light district, adjoining the **Landungsbrücken**; the **Erotic Art Museum** (www.eroticartmuseum.de; Sun–Thu noon–10pm, Fri–Sat noon–midnight) claims to be the largest of its kind in the world, and treats its subject with seriousness and taste, with exhibits from the 6th century to the present. While St Pauli's main thoroughfare, the **Reeperbahn**, certainly has its seedy side, its prostitutes, strip shows and sex shops are complemented by the city's greatest concentration of restaurants, bars, nightspots and other places of entertainment, all of which make it a magnet for all sorts of folk simply wanting a good evening out. Those who have partied all Saturday night tend to congregate early on Sunday mornings at the waterside **Fischmarkt**, a boisterous affair where all sorts of merchandise, not only fish, is bought and sold.

LÜBECK

Protected by formidable water defences, handsome **Lübeck** ❹ preserves the atmosphere of its glory days when it presided over the medieval Hanseatic League of trading cities and dominated the commerce of the Baltic and beyond. With no suitable stone at hand, the city was built of brick, and it was here that *Backsteingotik* originated, a striking variant of Gothic architecture whose influence can be seen all round the Baltic shores, from Rostock to Tallinn in far-off Estonia. The style encompassed the humblest dwelling as much as the grandest church, and gave the Hanse cities their wonderfully harmonious appearance, none more so than Lübeck. Grievous wartime destruction – a single air raid in 1942 destroyed a quarter of the city – has been made good, and Lübeck more than deserves the Unesco listing it was given in 1987.

The skills of Lübeck's builders are splendidly evident in the iconic structure guarding the main approach, the 15th-century gateway known as the Holstentor. Two sturdy brick towers are linked by a gatehouse containing an archway and topped by the typical stepped gables of *Backsteingotik*. Inside the gateway, the pride of the **Museum Holstentor** (www.die-luebecker-museen.de; Apr–Dec daily 10am–6pm, Jan–Mar Tue–Sun 11am–5pm) is a superb model of the city as it was in the 17th century. For a fine view over Lübeck and its setting near the mouth of the River Trave, head to the nearby **Petrikirche (St Peter's Church)**, whose viewing gallery (www.st-petri-luebeck.de; daily Apr–Sept 9am–8pm, Oct–Mar 10am–6pm) is accessible by lift.

Almost always crowded, with both visitors and locals, the city's marketplace is dominated by the **Rathaus** (town hall) and the **Marienkirche** (www.st-marien-luebeck.de daily Apr–Sept 10am–6pm,

Thomas Mann

Opposite the Marienkirche is Buddenbrookhaus (www.buddenbrookhaus.de; Tue–Sun Jan 11am–5pm, daily Feb–Mar 11am–5pm, Apr–Dec 10am–6pm), a shrine to Lübeck's literary lion, Thomas Mann (1875–1955), whose novel, *Buddenbrooks*, is set in the city.

Oct–Dec 10am–5pm, Jan–Mar 10am–4pm). The town hall's brickwork is extraordinarily elaborate, with dramatic circular openings in the upper walls to diminish wind resistance. The twin-towered church contains several works of art, and in one tower, two bells that crashed to the ground in the terrible air raid of 1942 have been left embedded in the floor of what is now a chapel as a memorial.

◉ THE HANSEATIC LEAGUE

The initial letters on German car licence plates reveal the locality where the plates were issued: B for Berlin, for instance. In northern Germany, many plates have a letter H preceding the town code: HH for Hamburg, HB for Bremen, HL for Lübeck, HR for Rostock. That first H is something these and other towns are inordinately proud of. It stands for Hansestadt (Hanseatic City), and recalls the city's membership in the Hanseatic League.

For nearly four centuries, from the 1200s to the 1600s, the Baltic-based federation of trading towns was an economic powerhouse. The wealth generated created prosperity across northern Europe, some at least of which trickled down from the merchants and city councillors who controlled the trade to the ordinary burghers. Trading profits paid for magnificent Gothic churches, town halls and civic and private buildings in the Hanseatic towns, many of them built of characteristic red *Backstein* (brick). Many of them can still be admired today.

For most of the league's existence, during which its tentacles spread from the Baltic heartland as far as London, Bruges, Bergen and Novgorod, Lübeck was its seat. If one single location may be said to define the Hanseatic period, it could be the Haus der Schiffergesellschaft, the city's seafarers' guildhouse.

A stroll around the streets and squares reveals many minor treasures, among them the 13th-century hospice called the **Heilig-Geist-Hospital**, and the **Haus der Schiffergesellschaft**, once the home of the seafarers' guild and now a popular restaurant. Lübeck is still a busy port, though its harbour is now at the mouth of the Trave. There, the elegant resort of **Travemünde** boasts fine beaches, fishermen's houses, seafood restaurants and a casino.

The far north

SCHLESWIG-HOLSTEIN AND THE NORTH SEA COAST

Other resorts stud the Baltic coast to the north, whose most characteristic features are narrow inlets leading inland to sheltered port towns.

The most important of these towns is **Kiel ❺**, once Imperial Germany's most important naval base, and now the capital of the *Land* of Schleswig-Holstein, a peninsula stretching north to the border with Denmark. Kiel is famous for the world's greatest sailing event, the regatta known as the *Kieler Woche* (Kiel Week), and has also given its name to the great shipping canal linking the North Sea and the Baltic. At the head of other inlets stand the towns of **Schleswig** and **Flensburg**. Schleswig's Renaissance Schloss Gottorf houses the Nydam Boat, a superb example of a Viking longship, while Flensburg,

The Bremen Town Musicians

Germany's northernmost city, has a unique atmosphere thanks to its substantial Danish minority.

The great attraction of Germany's North Sea coastline is its islands. Forming two distinct groups, they consist of the **Nordfriesische Inseln** (North Frisian Islands) stretching along the western coast of Schleswig-Holstein, parts of them protected by a national park, and the **Ostfriesische Inseln** (East Frisian Islands) off the coast of Lower Saxony. With sand dunes, abundant wildlife and glorious sandy beaches, all are popular with visitors, though it is only North Frisian **Sylt** and its glamorous capital Westerland that are well known internationally. East Frisian Borkum and Nordeney are equally bustling in summer, while smaller islands like Spiekeroog and Wangerooge are traffic-free and frequented by those who crave peace and quiet.

The island of **Helgoland** (Heligoland) is buttressed by red sandstone cliffs. This one-time British possession lies about 70km (44 miles) offshore and is reached from the port of Cuxhaven at the mouth of the Elbe. Cuxhaven is overshadowed by far larger **Bremerhaven**, a modern harbour town first developed in the 19th century. The magnificent **Deutsches Schiffahrtsmuseum** (National Maritime Museum; www.dsm.museum; Apr–Oct daily 10am–6pm, Nov–Mar Tue–Sun 10am–6pm) deals expertly with all aspects of Germany's relationship with the sea. The **Zoo am**

Meer Bremerhaven (https://zoo-am-meer-bremerhaven.de; daily Apr–Sept 9am–7pm, Mar and Oct 9am–6pm, Nov–Feb 9am–4.30pm) is a marine zoo specialising in Arctic fish and mammals.

Bremen

The ancient Hanseatic city of **Bremen** ❻ lies far inland up the River Weser. Like Hamburg, Bremen is a Federal *Land* in its own right, and is equally proud of its history, which goes back to the 8th century. Overlooked by the twin-towered St Petri-Dom, parts of which date from the 11th century, the city's focal point is its sprawling square, at its centre the grandiose **Rathaus** (Town Hall), a splendid example of Weser Renaissance architecture. A huge medieval figure of the knight Roland, the guardian of civic liberties, stands in the square, contrasting with a droll modern sculpture which has become a city emblem: the Bremen Town Musicians (Stadtmusikanten); a cockerel, cat, dog and donkey,

⊘ HIKING THE SEABED

Separating the North Frisian and East Frisian islands from the German mainland is the Wattenmeer (Wadden Sea). So shallow is this narrow body of water that when the tide is out, at many places along the coast the sea vanishes altogether. At such times, a hardy breed of adventurer steps out onto the exposed seabed and ploughs across the muddy bottom to the offshore islands. Known as *Wattwandern* or *Wattlaufen*, wandering or walking on the mudflats is not as crazy as it looks. It is in fact a highly organised activity, with groups led by licensed guides getting a close encounter with the seafloor and a look at what is generally hidden by a curtain of water, and will be again as soon as the next tide comes in.

which come from a folk tale popularised by the Brothers Grimm. The Weser waterfront, with its bars and restaurants, is reached from the square by the unusual Böttcherstrasse, a street laid out in the 1920s and '30s and flanked by brick buildings in Expressionist style. Among its shops and museums is the **Paula Modersohn-Becker Museum** (www.museen-boettcherstrasse. de; Tue–Sun 11am–6pm), named after the best-known painter from the early 20th-century artists' colony established in the nearby village of **Worpswede**. Bremen's other most attractive streets are in the **Schnoorviertel**, the picturesque and much-tidied-up former fisherfolk's quarter.

MECKLENBURG-LOWER POMERANIA

The lovely landscapes of the Mecklenburg lakeland begin within easy reach of Hamburg and Lübeck, and even **Schwerin ❼**, the capital of the *Land* of Mecklenburg-Vorpommern is only a short distance away. It is an aristocratic place, the former seat of the dukes of Mecklenburg, with a charming Altstadt, a *Backsteingotik* cathedral, and a fabulous ducal palace on an island in the Schweriner See, Germany's third-largest lake. The **Schweriner Schloss** (www.schloss-schwerin.de; Tue–Sun 10am–6pm, until 5pm mid-Oct to mid-Apr) is a fantastical con-glomeration of different architectural styles, from neo-Gothic to neo-baroque, with a tower, turret or pinnacle for every day of the year. As well as a sumptuous interior it has two superb gardens, the Burggarten and the Schlossgarten, the latter a masterpiece of baroque landscaping. East of Schwerin, the smaller, well-preserved town of **Güstrow** also has a ducal Schloss (www.museum-schwerin.de; Tue–Sun Apr–Oct 11am–6pm, Nov–Mar 11am–5pm), less ostentatious perhaps, but a fine example of genuine Renaissance architecture with a for-mal garden to match.

Linked to one another by rivers and canals, the countless bodies of water of the Mecklenburg lakeland are popular with boating enthusiasts. The most extensive lake, second only to Lake Constance in size, is the **Müritzsee**, approached from the attractive town of Waren. Part of the area is protected as a national park, its woods and marshes a haven for wildlife, including Germany's heraldic bird, the sea eagle.

Wismar marketplace

THE BALTIC COAST

Along the Baltic coast, splendid beaches and old-fashioned seaside resorts alternate with historic harbour towns. Like Lübeck, all the latter were once members of the Hanseatic League, and all share Lübeck's *Backsteingotik* atmosphere as well as having strong individual identities. **Wismar** is focused on its spacious marketplace, lined with gabled town mansions in various styles, at its centre the *Wassserkunst*, a domed Renaissance fountain. Beyond the one surviving city gateway is the Alter Hafen (Old Harbour), where a number of historic vessels are moored.

While Wismar was the GDR's second most important port, **Rostock** ❽ was promoted as the Communist state's main outlet to the world's oceans. A potential capital of Mecklenburg-Vorpommern, Rostock lost out in the end to Schwerin, but retains a livelier atmosphere than its competitor, particularly

Saxony's 'Little Switzerland'

along its bustling main street, traffic-free Kröpeliner Strasse. Parallel to it runs Lange Strasse, a broad boulevard rebuilt after wartime bombing in a curious Stalinist version of *Backsteingotik*. Plenty of museums and monuments compete for the visitor's attention, perhaps the most interesting being the **Schiffbau- und Schifffahrtsmuseum** (Shipbuilding and Maritime Museum; www.schifffahrtsmuseum-rostock. de; Apr–June, Sept–Oct Tue–Sun 10am–6pm, July–Aug daily 10am–6pm, Nov–Mar Tue–Sun 10am–4pm), which traces the city's relationship with the Baltic, with particular emphasis on the GDR period. In summer, the best way of getting to Rostock's seaside suburb of **Warnemünde**, with its promenade, cafés and restaurants, is by steamer along the wide River Warnow.

Some 70km (44 miles) to the east of Rostock and located on a superb natural harbour, compact **Stralsund ❾** has kept more of its original character than the other port cities. Its great Marienkirche is physically linked to its Rathaus, an extraordinary edifice with a great seven-gabled facade. The town has a museum of more than local importance, the excellent **Deutsches Meeresmuseum** (National Museum of the Sea; www.meeresmuseum.de; Apr–Oct daily 10am–5pm, Nov–Mar Tue–Sun 10am–5pm), which has no fewer than 45 aquariums. In recognition of their historical importance, Stralsund and Wismar have been given Unesco World Heritage status.

The heyday of the Baltic coast as a summer resort was in the period before World War I and in the interwar years. But the groundwork had been laid much earlier by aristocrats: in the 1790s, Grand Duke Friedrich of Mecklenburg built a delightful group of neoclassical holiday villas at **Heiligendamm**, while the small spa town of **Putbus** was laid out in 1810 on the island of **Rügen ⑩** by Prince Wilhelm Malte.

Rügen, which is reached from Stralsund, is Germany's largest island, with a wealth of things to visit, among them the **Nationalpark Jasmund**, with its gorgeous forests of beech and the sparkling white chalk cliffs immortalised in a painting by the early 19th-century artist Caspar David Friedrich.

The chain of resorts (Bansin, Heringsdorf, Ahlbeck) fringing the glorious beaches of **Usedom ⑪**, Germany's easternmost island, are still proud to call themselves *Kaiserbäder* (Imperial spas), a status given to them when they were patronised by Kaiser Wilhelm II and his court. Unlike the much redeveloped seaside resorts of western Germany, they and many of the other Baltic resorts have kept their period charm. Usedom's other great attraction is the **Historisch-Technisches Museum** (Historical Technology Museum; www.peenemuende.de; Apr–Sept daily 10am–6pm, Oct daily 10am–4pm, Nov–Mar Tue–Sun 10am–4pm) at **Peenemünde**, the base where the revolutionary V2 rocket was developed in World War II.

DRESDEN AND THE TWO SAXONYS

Until 1918 Saxony was a kingdom, and today's Land retains a strong sense of itself as a realm of some distinction, calling itself *Freistaat Sachsen* (the Free State of Saxony). The Saxon rulers were renowned for their extravagant love of the arts, and their capital Dresden, with its great monuments lovingly rebuilt after wartime devastation, once more deserves its title of 'Florence on the Elbe'. Just downstream from Dresden, the much smaller but almost perfectly preserved little city of Meissen was where a Saxon king's obsession with fine things led to the discovery of the secret of porcelain manufacture. The wealth and fame of Saxony's second great city, Leipzig, was created not by monarchs but by merchants, publishers, printers and musicians, foremost among the latter Johann Sebastian Bach. In 1989, it was here that the wave of popular protest gathered strength that led to the downfall of the East German Communist regime. Saxony has fine countryside, particularly in the upland areas along the border with the Czech Republic. Here, the Erzgebirge (Ore Mountains) are the home of long-standing mining traditions, while few of Germany's landscapes are as spectacular as the 300m (1,000ft) cliffs and rock formations towering over the Elbe in the national park known as Saxony's 'Little Switzerland' (Sächsische Schweiz).

The 'other Saxony', Sachsen-Anhalt, is a recent creation as a *Land*. Its capital, Magdeburg, has eastern Germany's finest medieval cathedral, while its rival, Halle, is proud of its musical traditions as well as boldly facing up to the problematic industrial heritage bequeathed by Communism. Dessau is famous as the home of the influential interwar Bauhaus school of design, while nearby is the World Heritage Site of Wörlitz, Germany's foremost landscape park.

The Dresden skyline at the Brühlsche Terrasse

DRESDEN

Demoted by the Communists to a mere district town, princely **Dresden** 🕑 is once more the capital of Saxony. While the city will never quite recover the allure it had before the Allied air raids of February 1945, the reconstruction of its great historic buildings has restored its famous skyline and its unparalleled artistic heritage draws visitors from all over the world.

Near the River

Perhaps the best place to begin an exploration of Dresden's wealth of attractions is to stroll along the **Brühlsche Terrasse**, the elevated promenade laid out along the banks of the Elbe. The terrace gives wonderful views of the river, graced by the big white pleasure steamers of the famous *Weisse Flotte* (White Fleet). On the far shore is the Neustadt, the elegant 18th-century town extension which was relatively unaffected by the bombing, and which now attracts the crowds to its shops, cafés, restaurants and nightlife. By the Altstadt end of the Augustusbrücke, the bridge named after Augustus the Strong, Saxony's most flamboyant monarch, stands the restored **Hofkirche**, the baroque court church. It was designed by an Italian architect, who imported numerous fellow countrymen to help in its construction, housing them in the **Italienisches Dörfchen** (Italian Village), now a popular riverside restaurant. The church abuts the **Residenzschloss** (www.skd.museum; Wed–Mon 10am–6pm), until 1918 the palace of Saxony's kings. With rebuilding almost complete, it now houses some of the city's most important collections, among them the **Kupferstich-Kabinett** (Museum of Prints and Drawings) with its half a million prints, drawings and photographs, and the **Grünes Gewölbe** (Green Vault), a sumptuous array of decorative objects on which Augustus squandered his kingdom's wealth. There's a fine panorama over the city centre from the palace's 100m (328ft) tower (end of Mar–early Nov Wed–Mon 10am–6pm).

Central Dresden

On the far side of Theaterplatz stands the **Semperoper** (Opera House), named after its architect, Gottfried Semper, and the scene of many a prestigious premiere, including operas by Wagner. Adjoining it is the **Zwinger**, perhaps the most stunning group of baroque buildings in Germany. Arranged around a spacious courtyard with lawns, pools and fountains, the Zwinger was built from 1709 onwards by Augustus's architect Pöppelmann to house the spendthrift monarch's collections and to be an appropriate setting for ostentatious pageants and festivities. The collections (www.skd.museum; Tue–Sun 10am–6pm) include the **Gemäldegalerie Alte Meister** (Old Masters' Gallery), which houses some of the world's finest

The opulent Zwinger

paintings including Raphael's emblematic *Sistine Madonna*; the fabulous **Porzellansammlung** (Porcelain Collection) and the **Rüstkammer** (Armoury); and the antique scientific instruments of the **Mathematisch-Physikalischer Salon** (Mathematical-Physical Sciences Saloon).

The counterpart to the Old Masters' Gallery is the **Galerie Neue Meister** (New Masters' Gallery; www.skd.museum; Tue–Sun 10am–6pm) in the **Albertinum**; here are works by some of Germany's greatest 19th- and 20th-century artists, among them one of the most searing condemnations of war ever painted, the triptych *Der Krieg* by Otto Dix. Symbolising Dresden's recovery from the horrors of war is the glorious domed **Frauenkirche** (Church of Our Lady), for decades a ruin, then rebuilt stone by numbered stone from 1994 onwards, and finally reconsecrated in late 2005. The gilded cross atop the dome was donated by Britain's 'Dresden Trust'.

The area around the Frauenkirche is scheduled to be rebuilt along traditional lines, respecting the old, irregular street pattern. By contrast, much of the post-war reconstruction of war-wrecked Dresden paid little attention to history, and the busy main shopping area, traffic-free **Prager Strasse**, is a Communist-era showpiece of unrelenting geometric regularity.

Outer Dresden

Some of the atmosphere of the prewar city lingers in the elegant villa quarters of the suburbs and in open spaces such as the vast **Grosser Garten**, one of Germany's foremost urban parks. On the edge of the park is one of the country's most unusual museums, the **Deutsches Hygiene-Museum** (www. dhmd.de; Tue–Sun 10am–6pm), its most prized exhibit the 'Glass Human', with a completely transparent body. Some of the loveliest vistas of Dresden are from the heights above the River Elbe just upstream from the centre; they can be reached from the suburb of Loschwitz by funicular and cable railway.

⊙ THE SORBS

Visitors to southeastern Germany are sometimes surprised to find bilingual road signs, pointing, for example, to Bautzen – Budyšin. The latter is the name used for the city by the Sorbs, a Slav minority of some 50,000 people who have somehow managed to preserve their language and culture despite being surrounded and overwhelmingly outnumbered by Germans. Colourful Sorbian traditions include Zapust, several days of festivities at Shrovetide, while Easter is marked by horseback processions and intricately painted Easter eggs.

AROUND DRESDEN

The impact of Augustus the Strong was felt far beyond the city limits. His pleasure palaces in the countryside include the huge hunting lodge of **Schloss Moritzburg** (www. schloss-moritzburg.de; Mar–Nov daily 10am–6pm, Dec–Feb Tue–Sun 10am–5pm, closed 26 Feb–19 Mar, 5 Nov–16 Nov, 24 and 31 Dec), 14km (9 miles) northwest of Dresden. Rising from the middle of

Meissen is known for its fine porcelain

a great artificial lake on which lavish water pageants were held, it has an interior crammed with trophies of the chase. Upstream from the city and best reached by pleasure steamer, the mock-Chinese extravaganza of **Schloss Pillnitz** (www. schlosspillnitz.de; Mar–Nov daily 9am–6pm, Nov–Apr Sat–Sun guided tours 11am–2pm; the palace park open all year until dusk; Bergpalais closed Mon, Wasserpalais closed Tue) stands among the vineyards rising from the riverbank. It makes a fine home for a superlative decorative arts collection.

The steamer continues upstream from Pillnitz to the historic town of **Pirna**, then passes beneath the most spectacular feature of the national park **Sächsische Schweiz** (Saxony's 'Little Switzerland'), the crags and pinnacles of the **Bastei** rock. The panorama from the Bastei, with its vertiginous viewpoints, is one of the most sensational in Germany, taking in the winding river far below as well as other imposing rock

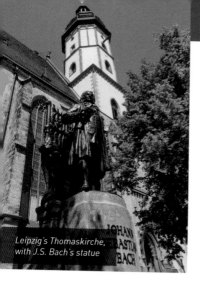
Leipzig's Thomaskirche, with J.S. Bach's statue

formations, one of them crowned by the great fortress of **Königstein**.

Most trippers leave the steamer at the spa town of **Bad Schandau**, though it is possible to carry on into the Czech Republic. Less dramatic than Saxon Switzerland, but still with many charms, the well-wooded upland countryside along the Czech border is a paradise for walkers and the less ambitious winter sports enthusiast. Known as the **Lausitz**, and once part of the Czech kingdom, it has its own miniature capital in the shape of **Bautzen ⓭**. This 1,000-year-old, many-towered city built above the winding River Spree is the cultural centre of the Sorb minority, and its castle, the Ortenburg, is the home of the **Serbski Muzej** (Sorbian Museum; http://sorbisches-museum. de; Tue–Sun 10am–6pm). Bautzen was notorious for its harsh prison, the **Bautzen II**, now a memorial to people who suffered under the Nazi and Communist regimes (www.stsg.de/cms/ bautzen/startseite; Mon–Thu 10am–4pm, Fri 10am–8pm, Sat– Sun 10am–6pm; free).

Separated from Poland only by the River Neisse, **Görlitz ⓮**, 39km (24 miles) east of Bautzen, miraculously survived World War II with little damage. Its extensive Altstadt, which features wonderful medieval churches and Renaissance mansions, is one of the best preserved in Germany.

Downstream along the Elbe from Dresden, **Meissen ⓑ** is dominated by its cathedral and castle, the **Albrechtsburg**, built on the rocky bluff overlooking the river. It was while confined to the castle that Augustus's court alchemist discovered the technique of making perfect porcelain. The streets, squares and alleyways of the old town are a delight to explore, but most visitors come here for the **Staatliche Porzellan-Manufaktur** (State Porcelain Factory; www.meissen.com; daily 9am–6pm, until 5pm in winter), to see craftspeople at work and marvel at the historic porcelain in the museum.

Schloss Colditz (www.schloss-colditz.com; Apr–Oct daily 10am–5pm, Nov–Mar 10am–4pm) is just one of several castles along the picturesque River Mulde, but owes its near-mythical status to its role as a prison for incorrigible Allied escapers in World War II. A tour reveals the extraordinary ingenuity of those confined here, 30 of whom succeeded in making 'home runs' from the supposedly escape-proof fortress.

LEIPZIG

Mercantile **Leipzig ⓰** makes little attempt to compete with Dresden in terms of glamour and great monuments. It's a workaday city, whose historic buildings reflect civic pride rather than aristocratic ambition. Typical is the **Altes Rathaus** (Old Town Hall; www.stadtgeschichtliches-museum-leipzig.de; Tue–Sun 10am–6pm), with its

J.S. Bach in Leipzig

Bach's works were neglected after his death, and the revival of his reputation only came during the 19th century, thanks to the efforts of Felix Mendelssohn, who conducted Leipzig's renowned Gewandhaus orchestra between 1835 and 1845. With its fine acoustics, today's Gewandhaus building is one of the more distinguished edifices of the Communist era.

steep roof, clock tower and distinctive gables. Run up astonishingly quickly in the space of a few months in 1556 in the interval between two of Leipzig's famous trade fairs, it now houses the city museum and a superb ceremonial hall graced by portraits of city fathers.

All around are the arcades which have long been a feature of Leipzig; once used to display the wares of merchants attending the fairs, they now make it possible to shop your way around the city almost entirely under cover. In one of the arcades, the **Mädlerpassage**, is **Auerbachs Keller**, the vaulted basement pub which was the scene of a dramatic episode in Goethe's Faust. Goethe had many connections with Leipzig, and his statue stands in the **Naschmarkt** in front of the old stock exchange, the city's loveliest baroque building.

But the man most people associate with Leipzig has to be Johann Sebastian Bach. In 1723 Bach was appointed city musician and choirmaster of the 13th century **Thomaskirche** (Church of St Thomas). The celebrated boys' choir, the Thomaner, still sing. Their former master is buried in his church, and his statue stands outside, opposite the **BachMuseum** (www.bachmuseumleipzig.de; Tue–Sun 10am–5pm).

As well as the Thomaskirche, Leipzig has another landmark church, the **Nikolaikirche** (Church of St Nicholas), a Romanesque structure given a highly original, gloriously ornate interior in the late 18th century. In the 1980s, it served as a refuge for opponents of the GDR regime, and in 1989 it was the rallying point for the great demonstrations which led to the government's collapse.

The story of what Leipzig's resisters were up against is compellingly told in the **Museum in der 'Runden Ecke'** (Museum in the 'Round Corner'; www.runde-ecke-leipzig.de; daily 10am–6pm; free), the former Stasi secret police headquarters, while the daily

The Kornhaus restaurant in Dessau

realities of life under Communism are evoked in the displays of the **Zeitgeschichtliches Forum** (Contemporary History Forum; www.hdg.de; Tue–Fri 9am–6pm, Sat–Sun from 10am; free).

There's plenty more to see in Leipzig; if you have come here by train, you will already have admired the huge railway station, said to be the largest terminus in the world. Even more colossal is the granite **Völkerschlachtdenkmal** (www.voelkerschlachtdenkmal.eu; daily Apr–Oct 10am–6pm, Nov–Mar 10am–4pm), the monument to the Battle of the Nations, which took place outside the city in 1813. Erected exactly a century later, this man-made mountain is the perfect embodiment of the bombastic, militaristic spirit of Kaiser Wilhelm's Germany.

LUTHERSTADT WITTENBERG
The Leipzig–Berlin train pauses briefly at **Lutherstadt Wittenberg**, an otherwise modest town so proud of its

Bauhaus main building, Dessau

associations with Martin Luther that it has incorporated his name into its official title. It was here that Luther nailed his 95 theses to the door of the castle's church, and there are many sights connected with him. Foremost among them is the **Lutherhaus** (www.martinluther.de; Apr–Oct daily 9am–6pm, Nov–Mar Tue–Sun 10am–5pm), with its museum of the Reformation. In the Unesco Biosphere Reserve Mittlere Elbe downstream from Wittenberg spreads the parkland of **Wörlitz**, laid out in the late 18th century for Prince Leopold of Anhalt-Dessau. It is perhaps Germany's supreme achievement in landscape design, with lakes, pavilions, gazebos, romantic ruins and lavish planting.

Prince Leopold and the other rulers of Anhalt-Dessau beautified their capital, **Dessau** ⓱, which was devastated in World War II. The city is remembered today mostly as the seat of the hugely influential design school of the interwar period, the **Bauhaus**. Its pioneering main building, all glass, steel and concrete, designed by Walter Gropius, still stands, a magnet for design students and enthusiasts (www.bauhaus-dessau. de; daily 10am–5pm). Among Dessau's other examples of Modernist architecture are the **Meisterhäuser**, cuboid residences built for the Bauhaus professors and, on the banks of the Elbe, the panoramic **Kornhaus** restaurant.

MAGDEBURG AND HALLE

Astride the River Elbe and the main routes from western Germany to Berlin, **Magdeburg** enjoys a favourable location which may have been decisive when it was chosen as the capital of Sachsen-Anhalt against fierce competition from Halle. The city's origins go back to the early Middle Ages, when the Elbe was the frontier between Germans and Slavs, and Magdeburg became a great centre of German-Christian missionary work and conquest. Little remains of the historic town, destroyed in successive sieges and wars, but over everything still rises the superb twin-towered **Dom**, a Gothic cathedral with an interior rich in sculpture of all periods.

Magdeburg's rival, **Halle ⓲**, 29km (18 miles) to the north-west of Leipzig, is the larger of the two cities, a bustling place centred on its irregular Marktplatz dominated by the landmark Roter Turm (Red Tower) and the four spires of the Marktkirche. The city's most famous son, Georg Friedrich Händel, played the organ here, and his life and work are celebrated in his

⦿ WEIMAR CLASSICISM

That size really doesn't matter is proved by the way in which little Weimar, with its tiny ducal court, became the cultural capital of Germany in the late 18th and early 19th century. The genial figures of Schiller and Goethe bestrode the intellectual currents of the age, producing literature that, like Shakespeare's works, is of universal appeal and significance and cannot be contained within any single category. As well as a prodigious output of poetry, novels and plays like Faust, Goethe made valuable contributions to the natural sciences, while Schiller is best known for historical dramas like *Maria Stuart* which have enjoyed a revival in English translation.

birthplace, the **Händel-Haus** (www.haendelhaus.de; Tue–Sun Apr–Oct 10am–6pm, Nov–Mar 10am–5pm). Halle's notoriously polluting chemical industries have either gone out of business or been cleaned up; their origins go back centuries to the discovery of saline springs, and an intriguing and unusual attraction is the old saltworks, now the **Technisches Halloren- und Salinemuseum** (www.salinemuseum.de; Tue–Sun 10am–5pm).

WEIMAR AND THURINGIA

At the geographical heart of Germany, the *Land* of Thüringen (Thuringia) seems to distil the very essence of the country. Stately old towns are strung along the Via Regia, the ancient highway leading east–west across the province; there are ancient castles and churches galore, while to the south stretch the wonderfully wooded uplands of the Thuringian Forest. Farmland abounds and, just over the border in Sachsen-Anhalt, vineyards flourish along the course of the River Saale. While the capital of classical German culture, Weimar, has always drawn visitors from around the globe, the rest of Thuringia has remained relatively unknown. Nowadays, however, more and more people are discovering its attractions.

WEIMAR

This modest little city still seems to breathe the harmonious atmosphere of the golden age in Germany's cultural history known as Weimar Classicism. **Weimar** ⑲ is indissolubly associated with the name of that universal genius, Johann Wolfgang von Goethe (1749–1832), who for most of his life served as a privy councillor of Carl August, enlightened ruler of the little duchy of Saxony-Weimar-Eisenach. Goethe attracted other luminaries here like his friend and fellow playwright Friedrich

Schiller. Other figures who flourished at Weimar, both before and after Goethe's time, include the painter Lucas Cranach the Elder, the poet Christoph-Martin Wieland, and the philosopher Johann Gottfried Herder. Bach was court musician for a while, as was Liszt, and Nietzsche spent the last part of his life in Weimar. In 1919 the Bauhaus design school started here, and the city gave its name to the ill-

Goethe and Schiller in Weimar

fated interwar Weimar Republic, whose parliament drew up its democratic constitution here at a safe distance from Berlin, which was racked by revolutionary disturbance.

Weimar has no grandiose monuments, and the best way to experience the town is to wander its streets at random, perhaps beginning at the **Deutsches Nationaltheater** (German National Theatre), fronted by a famous statue of Goethe and Schiller. One compulsory stop is **Goethes Wohnhaus** (Goethe's House; www.klassik-stiftung.de; Tue–Sun Apr–Oct 9.30am–6pm, Nov–Mar 9.30am–4pm). The original house, with its many poignant reminders of the great man, is adjoined by an excellent modern museum devoted to his life and times. Goethe was fascinated by landscape, and helped lay out the lovely **Park an der Ilm** with its garden retreat known as **Goethes Gartenhaus**.

About 8km (5 miles) to the north of the city is **Buchenwald** concentration camp, established by the Nazis in 1937. Named after the area's abundant beech woods, Buchenwald was not an extermination camp as such, though by the end of World War II more than 50,000 people had perished here. A further 10,000 deaths occurred in the immediate post-war period. The remains of the camp are now the **Gedenkstätte Buchenwald** (Buchenwald Memorial; www.buchenwald.de; Tue–Sun Apr–Oct 10am–6pm, Nov–Mar 10am–4pm; free).

ERFURT, GOTHA AND EISENACH

The Via Regia leads westwards from Weimar to well-preserved **Erfurt ⑳**, the capital of Thuringia and one of the great cities of medieval Germany. Among the many things to see is the **Krämerbrücke** (Merchants' Bridge), a medieval river crossing lined with shops, but the most striking sight in Erfurt is that of

Erfurt architecture

its two great churches loom-
ing high above the spacious
Domplatz; the **Severikirche**
with its spiky steeples is
impressive enough, but the
cathedral's proportions are
truly stunning. Its treasures
include the huge Gloriosa
bell, superb stained glass
and a triangular porch
adorned with sculptures of
the Wise and Foolish Virgins.

> **Cars in Eisenach**
>
> Automobil Welt Eisenach
> (Automobile World; www.
> awe-stiftung.de; Tue–Sun
> 10am–6pm, until 5pm in
> winter) reflects the city's
> long association with car
> manufacturing. Exhibits
> include the nearest thing
> the GDR had to a prestige
> vehicle, the Wartburg.

Further along the east–west highway stands the little city of
Gotha, once the seat of the Saxe-Coburg-Gotha dynasty which
provided monarchs for much of Europe, including Britain, and
which gave its name to the *Who's Who* of German aristocracy,
the *Almanac de Gotha*. The charming old town, with its delightful red Renaissance Rathaus, crouches at the foot of the rise
crowned by gigantic **Schloss Friedenstein** (www.stiftung
friedenstein.de; Tue–Sun 10am–5pm, until 4pm in winter).
Built in the mid-17th century, the great ducal residence with
its formidable corner towers has a sumptuous interior housing
the extensive collections assembled by successive dukes, as
well as an original baroque theatre.

The westernmost of Thuringia's string of cities, almost on the
border with Hessen, **Eisenach** ㉑ attracts visitors in their thousands. Most come here to marvel at the **Wartburg** (www.wart-
burg-eisenach.de; Apr–Oct daily 8.30am–5pm, Nov–Mar daily
9am–3.30pm), the 11th-century stronghold perched atop the
last spur of the Thuringian Forest above the town. Everyone's
idea of what a German castle should be like, the Wartburg is rich
in romantic associations and in the 19th century became a great

The Wartburg, Thuringia's mighty stronghold

symbol of German nationalism, when it was zealously restored. Earlier it had been a refuge for Martin Luther, who completed his translation of the Bible here; a mark on the wall of his study is supposed to be the result of his hurling his inkpot at the devil.

Luther is remembered in Eisenach itself, where he lodged as a schoolboy in what is now the **Lutherhaus** (www.lutherhaus-eisenach.com; Apr–Oct daily 10am–5pm, Nov–Mar Tue–Sun 10am–5pm) and where he later preached in the **Georgenkirche**. But the city's most famous son is J.S. Bach, born in the **Bachhaus** (bachhaus.de; daily 10am–6pm), now 600 years old, which has a fine collection of antique musical instruments.

THURINGIAN FOREST

There are fine views of the forested uplands of the **Thüringer Wald** (Thuringian Forest) from Wartburg Castle, as well as from the nearby **Burschenschaftsdenkmal** (Fraternities Memorial), erected to mark a great rally of patriotic students in 1817. One of central Germany's favourite holiday and recreation areas, the Thuringian Forest rises to a height of nearly 1,000m (3,280ft) near the ski resort of Oberhof, but the best vistas are from the Grosser Inselberg, 916m (3,005ft) high above the little summer resort and spa of Tabarz. Keen hikers will tackle the famous long-distance trail of the **Rennweg**, a ridge-walk running the whole 100km (60-mile) length of the forest, while admirers of Goethe will want to follow in his footsteps to the countryside he loved around the old town of **Ilmenau**.

Arising in the eastern part of the Thuringian Forest, and with its upper reaches marked by a series of dams and reservoirs, the River Saale winds its way past picturesque small towns like **Saalfeld** and **Rudolstadt**. Close to Saalfeld are caves with astonishing concretions, the **Feengrotten** (Fairy Grottoes; www.feengrotten.de; May–Oct daily 10am–5pm, Nov–Dec and Feb–Apr daily 11am–3.30pm, Jan closed, Grottoneum 11am–3.30pm), considered to be the most colourful in the world.

The Saale flows north to the city of **Jena**, Thuringia's scientific counterpart to literary Weimar, as much identified with the 19th-century optical genius Carl Zeiss as the latter is with Goethe. Dominated by the cylindrical skyscraper of the university, Jena is still very much a centre of the optical and other hi-tech industries, whose origins are traced in the **Optisches Museum** (Museum of Optics; www.optischesmuseum.de; Tue–Fri 10am–4.30pm, Sat 11am–5pm). Continuing northwards over the border into Sachsen-Anhalt, the Saale is joined by its tributary the Unstrut.

The valley's combination of suitable soils and a favourable microclimate explains the presence here of Europe's northernmost vineyard, centred on the historic wine town of Freyberg and on the larger cathedral city of **Naumburg** ㉒. Its distinctive four-towered profile visible from far away, Naumburg's Dom

(Cathedral) is a splendid synthesis of Romanesque and Gothic architecture, though its great fame rests on its sculptures, particularly the noble couple known as Ekkehardt and Uta, the embodiment of the Germanic ideal of medieval chivalry.

HANOVER AND THE HARZ

While Hanover wears a resolutely modern face, and is more famous for its trade fairs than its historic heritage, this region of central Germany has a wealth of ancient and well-preserved towns. Hameln (Hamelin), whose children were spirited away by the sound of the Ratcatcher's flute, is a delight, as is timber-framed Goslar, the gateway to the Harz, the country's highest range of mountains north of the Alps, much of which is a national park. Less spectacular, the low-lying countryside north of Hanover includes the rolling, sandy expanses of Lüneburg Heath, bounded by the fine old cities of Lüneburg and Celle.

Dig deep

For 1,000 years, the Harz Mountains were exploited for their mineral wealth, yielding copper, lead, tin, zinc, silver and gold. The region's mining traditions can be investigated in the Bergbaumuseum Rammelsberg (Mining Museum; www.rammelsberg.de; Apr–Oct daily 9am–6pm, Nov–Mar 9am–5pm), just outside Goslar.

HANOVER

The capital of the *Land* of Lower Saxony (Niedersachsen), and the former seat of the dynasty that gave England a royal line in the 18th century, **Hannover** ㉓ (Hanover) no longer has a princely palace, thanks to bombing in World War II. But its **Grosser Garten** (Great Garden) survives; it is one of the great glories of baroque landscape design, linked to other historic parks, known collectively as the **Herrenhäuser Gärten** (Herrenhausen Gardens), by an avenue of lime trees and featuring a fountain spurting a jet of water 80m (260ft) into the air. On the far, southeastern side of the rebuilt city centre, there is another kind of open space, even more popular with locals: the **Maschsee**; the lake's waters make a fine foil to Hanover's most prominent

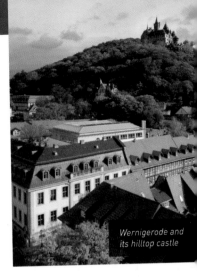

Wernigerode and its hilltop castle

public building, the **Neues Rathaus** (New City Hall). Completed in 1913, it has a flamboyant, neo-baroque exterior concealing opulent Art Nouveau interiors. The tower can be ascended by an inclined elevator for an overall view of the city in its green setting. Post-war Hanover profited from Leipzig's disappearance behind the Iron Curtain to become West Germany's leading centre of trade fairs, the extensive grounds of which have their own mainline rail station. The city's status was enhanced by the international Expo held here in 2000, Germany's first.

HAMELN AND HILDESHEIM

South of Hanover, the valley of the winding River Weser leads upstream through ever more attractive countryside. The river has given its name to a style of architecture known as 'Weser Renaissance', nowhere more splendidly exemplified than in **Hameln**, its old streets lined with exuberantly decorated, high-gabled town mansions. Better known in English as Hamelin, the town stages a pageant (on Sundays from mid-May to mid-Sept) celebrating the story of the infamous *Rattenfänger*, the stranger who rid the town first of its rats, then, when the city fathers withheld his fee, of its children.

There's more fine architecture in **Hildesheim**, though virtually every building on its Marktplatz is a reconstruction following near-total wartime destruction. But the town's greatest treasure is its heritage of Romanesque church architecture, protected by a Unesco World Heritage designation. It includes the perfectly preserved Godehardikirche, the Michaeliskirche with its painted ceiling, and the Dom, with its extraordinary 11th-century bronze doors depicting episodes from the Old and New Testaments.

HARZ MOUNTAINS

Visitors heading for the mountains of the Harz are strongly recommended to take a break in the old Imperial town of **Goslar**. A stroll around the cobbled streets reveals ever-changing

⊙ WALPURGISNACHT

In the Harz, the hours before dawn on 1 May are known as 'Walpurgis Night' or the 'Witches' Sabbath'. Legend has it that this is the time when witches gather on the Hexentanz-platz above Thale, before flying to the top of the Brocken on brooms, dung-forks and even tomcats. Here they dance wildly with each other before mating with the Devil, who confirms their magic powers. The legend gained credibility when Goethe made use of it in *Faust*, and nowadays the eve of Mayday is celebrated with abandon in towns and villages all around the Harz by thousands of costumed 'devils' and 'witches'.

compositions formed by an array of 1,000 or so ancient dwellings, most of them timber-framed and many featuring a wealth of carved detail. None is more charming than the imposing early 16th-century magistrate's residence known as the Brusttuch, now a hotel. Of a different order altogether is the Kaiserpfalz, the Imperial palace originally erected in the 11th century and comprehensively restored

Heather on the Lüneburg Heath

in the 1870s as a symbol of the newly united German Empire.

Visitors come to the Harz for the region's fresh air, hiking trails and broad vistas. Nowhere is the panorama more spectacular than from the rounded summit of the **Brocken**, at 1,142m (3,747ft) the highest point in central Germany. The Brocken features strongly in German myth, legend and literature, not least because of the way Goethe evoked its Walpurgisnacht in his *Faust*.

The mountain can be admired from the popular viewpoint of **Torfhaus**, where there is a national park information centre. Any number of trails lead to the summit; the easy way up is by the narrow-gauge trains of the Brockenbahn, hauled by magnificent steam engines built specially for this demanding job.

In GDR times, the Brocken – lying on the border with West Germany – was forbidden territory, with the Stasi deploying elaborate listening equipment on top of it, able to pick up 'capitalist' conversations many kilometres away. Their spying

Quedlinburg's timber-framed houses

paraphernalia has been succeeded by the Brockenhaus (www.
nationalpark-harz.de; daily 9.30am–5pm), a museum explaining the history and ecology of the mountain. An easy walk
leads round the summit, past strange rock formations where
witches are said to consort with the Devil.

There are plenty of pleasant resorts in and around the Harz,
but perhaps more interesting are towns like **Wernigerode**, with its
timber-framed buildings and extraordinarily picturesque old town
hall. To the southeast is the rather run-down industrial town of
Thale, a base for exploration of the rocky ravine of the River Bode,
which penetrates the very heart of the mountains. High above the
gorge is the Hexentanzplatz (Witches' Dancing Place) viewpoint,
reached by a short but spectacular trip in a cable car.

In the flat agricultural country to the east of the mountains
stands **Quedlinburg** ㉔. Few places exude quite the same sense
of Germany's deep history as this small town, overlooked by its

Burgberg, the hilltop citadel whose church contains a fabulous treasury and the tomb of King Heinrich I, the country's earliest king. The stone and timber-framed houses lining the lanes and streets below make up one of the finest collections of medieval and later buildings in the country. The whole of old Quedlinburg is deservedly a Unesco World Heritage Site.

AROUND LÜNEBURG HEATH

About 50km (30 miles) to the northwest of Hanover is the **Lüneburger Heide** (Lüneburg Heath), a vast tract of what was once continuous forest, but which human activity has converted over the centuries into a mosaic of farmland, woodland and pastureland grazed by a unique breed of sheep, the Heidschnucken. Sections of the area are protected as nature parks, and the heath has become increasingly popular with walkers, riders and wildlife enthusiasts. The Nazis located one of their more notorious concentration camps here; the liberation of **Bergen-Belsen** in early 1945 brought home to the world

⊘ LIVE STEAM

Steam railways are very much alive in the former GDR, many of them having been preserved for their usefulness and not just for sentimental reasons. Holidaymakers on Rügen are carried around by 'Rasender Roland' (Rushing Roland), while 'Molli' steams through the streets of the spa of Bad Doberan on her way to the coastal resorts of Heiligendamm and Kühlungsborn. There are also several steam railways in Saxony. But the most impressive steam line of all is the 110km (70-mile) Harz railway, a branch of which chugs valiantly all the way to the summit of the Brocken mountain (see page 79).

the horrors of the Nazi regime. The camp, on the west side of the Heath, is now a memorial site.

Celle, at the southern edge of the Heath, was a ducal seat and wears an aristocratic air. Its **Schloss** (www.celle-tourismus.de; Apr–Oct Tue, Fri and Sun for hourly guided tours 11am, 1pm, and 3pm, Nov–Mar Tue–Fri tours at 11am and 3pm, Sat–Sun tours at 11am, 1pm, and 3pm) contains a lovely Renaissance chapel and a baroque theatre. As well as hundreds of timber-framed dwellings, the town is also graced by a Rathaus in exuberant Weser Renaissance style. Celle is the German capital of equestrianism, the home of the State Stud Farm of Lower Saxony and of a splendid September parade of stallions.

North of the Heath and close to Hamburg, the town of **Lüneburg** is well worth a visit, its fine brick buildings reflecting its past connections with the Hanseatic cities of the coast. The town's prosperity depended on its salt deposits, and the old saltworks have been converted into the **Deutsches Salzmuseum** (National Salt Museum; www.salzmuseum.de; daily 10am–5pm).

LEMGO

Just over the border in the *Land* of North-Rhine Westfalia, **Lemgo** ㉕ was spared wartime damage and ranks among the most picturesque of the country's smaller towns, with an outstanding roster of late medieval and early Renaissance dwellings. Among them is the **Hexenbürgermeisterhaus** (House of the Witches' Mayor), home to a 16th-century mayor horribly zealous in his pursuit of witches; he sent dozens of innocent women to their death.

Not far from Lemgo, the hills and forests of the **Teutoburger Wald** are said to be the site of the great battle of AD9 in which the German chieftain Hermann won a great victory over the Roman legions sent against him.

Cologne Cathedral and the splendid railway bridge crossing the Rhine

COLOGNE, THE RUHR AND RHINE

The westernmost part of Germany is one of the most densely populated parts of the country. The great cities like Cologne and Düsseldorf, and the industrial centres of the Ruhr, all have their own distinct identities and range of attractions. Once the boundary of the Roman Empire, the Rhine remains one of Germany's great tourist attractions, especially where it has cut a spectacular winding gorge between Bingen and Koblenz. The valley of the Mosel is hardly less scenic. Less dramatic, the flat and watery landscapes around Münster, the old capital of Westphalia, invite quiet exploration.

COLOGNE

A great city in Roman times, and, in the Middle Ages, Germany's largest, **Köln** 26 (Cologne) is dominated by its glorious twin-towered cathedral, one of the supreme achievements of Gothic architecture. Repeatedly bombed in World War II, Cologne preserved its historic street pattern when it was rebuilt and, although most buildings are modern, much of its traditional atmosphere survives. It's a lively, humorous, rather disrespectful place, best experienced – for those with stamina – during the merrymaking of Karneval time (see box below). The historic core of Cologne is large, bounded by the semi-circular boulevard of the *Ring* running along the line of the old city walls, but the epicentre of city life is in the busy squares around the cathedral and the main railway station.

Kölner Dom and the Altstadt

Although construction of **Kölner Dom** (Cologne Cathedral; www.koelner-dom.de; Mon–Sat May–Oct 6am–9pm, Nov–Apr 6am–7.30pm, Sun (all year round) 1–4.30pm, except during services;

⊘ KARNEVAL IN COLOGNE

The arrival of Lent is greeted in Cologne, the rest of the Rhineland and other Roman Catholic parts of Germany with an outburst of merrymaking equalled only by Mardi Gras in warmer climes. The fun starts on the evening of the Thursday before Ash Wednesday, when women in fancy dress roam the streets, harassing any men foolish enough to show themselves. The tempo of events reaches a climax the following Monday – *Rosenmontag* – with a monster parade through the streets. Presiding over the celebrations is His Dottiness the Prince, attended by a Peasant and a (usually rather masculine) Virgin and hordes of costumed revellers. By Ash Wednesday the participants are well prepared for their 40 days of abstinence.

charge to tower) began in the 13th century, the building was only completed at the end of the 19th century, albeit in faithful adherence to the original medieval drawings which had somehow survived. The steeples rise to an astonishing 157m (515ft), and it takes more than 500 steps to reach the viewing platform on the south tower. The interior has a fabulous array of ecclesiastical treasures; they include the poignant

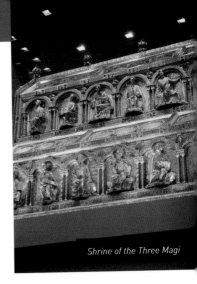

Shrine of the Three Magi

10th-century Cross of Gero showing Christ at the moment of death, the ornate Shrine of the Three Magi, and an altar painting by Cologne's greatest medieval painter, Stefan Lochner.

Flanking the cathedral's south front is the **Römisch-Germanisches Museum** (Roman-Germanic Museum; www.museenkoeln.de; Tue–Sun 10am–5pm). Well displayed items tell the story of this important frontier outpost of the Roman Empire, prominent among them the Dionysus Mosaic, made up of more than a million pieces and one of the finest of its kind anywhere.

From near the cathedral, Hohe Strasse follows the course of a Roman road southwards. Between it and the Rhine stretches the restored Altstadt, with its countless pubs, bars and restaurants, as well as surviving monuments like the Rathaus with its medieval towers, the Jewish *Mikwe* or ritual bath, and Gross St Martin, one of the city's Romanesque churches. At the heart of the Altstadt is the postmodern structure housing the splendid

Romanesque Gross St Martin

Wallraf das Museum (www.wallraf.museum; Tue–Sun 10am–6pm), whose prize exhibits are pictures by the late-medieval painters of the Cologne School, among them Lochner's masterpiece, the exquisite *Madonna in the Rose Garden*.

The city's other great art gallery is the vast **Museum Ludwig** (www.museum-ludwig.de; Tue–Sun 10am–6pm) overlooking the Rhine. It's one of the best galleries of modern art in Germany, and its collection of American painting – Warhol, Rothko, Rauschenberg – is unsurpassed. A walkway leads from here along the great railway bridge over the Rhine, giving an unbeatable view of the city's waterfront and the elaborate eastern end of the cathedral.

Two of Cologne's more unusual museums are the **Schokoladenmuseum** (www.schokoladenmuseum.de; Mon–Fri 10am–6pm, Sat–Sun 11am–7pm), devoted to chocolate, and the **Deutsches Sport- und Olympia-Museum** (National Sport and Olympics Museum; www.sportmuseum.info; Tue–Fri 10am–6pm, Sat–Sun 11am–7pm), with plenty of interactive exhibits.

Brühl

Only a short distance from Cologne, the town of **Brühl** offers contrasting possibilities for a day out. **Phantasialand** (www.phantasialand.de; mid-Mar–June and Sept–Oct daily

10am–6pm, Dec and beginning of Jan 11am–8pm, July–Aug 9am–8pm) is one of Germany's biggest theme parks. **Schloss Augustusburg** (www.schlossbruehl.de; Feb–Nov Tue–Fri 9am–noon, 1.30–4pm, Sat–Sun 10am–5pm) rivals any of southern Germany's baroque palaces in sheer sumptuousness, with a truly stunning park and gorgeous interiors.

BONN

Chosen in 1949 as the capital of West Germany, this medium-sized university town keenly felt its loss of status when Berlin became the seat of parliament after reunification in 1990. But **Bonn** ㉗ managed to keep some central-government functions and it has an array of museums and other attractions worthy of a far bigger city. It's also the birthplace of Beethoven, and makes much of the connection; the **Beethoven-Haus** (www.beethoven-haus-bonn.de; Apr–Oct daily 10am–6pm, Nov–Mar Mon–Sat 10am–5pm, Sun 11am–5pm) is a worthy shrine for the great composer's many fans, with evocative items like his love letters and ear trumpet. The streets and squares of Bonn's Altstadt contain many charming old buildings, but the dominant edifices are the pastel-coloured baroque Rathaus and the late Romanesque **Münster** (Minster), with its five towers. To the south are the city's modern museums, strung out along the 'Museum Mile'.

The **Kunstmuseum** (Art Gallery; www.kunstmuseum-bonn.de; Tue–Sun 11am–6pm, Wed until 9pm) is worth visiting for its holdings of works by local Expressionist August Macke. But a perhaps more compelling attraction is the **Haus der Geschichte der Bundesrepublik Deutschland** (House of the History of the Federal Republic of Germany; www.hdg.de/stiftung; Tue–Fri 9am–7pm, Sat–Sun 10am–6pm; free). The museum's excellent displays bring to life the story of the two Germanys in the post-war period.

AACHEN

Close to the border with the Netherlands and Belgium, Germany's westernmost city was chosen in AD794 by King of the Franks Charlemagne as the capital of his empire, not least because of his appreciation of the beneficial effects of its thermal springs. **Aachen** ㉘ is still a spa town, with superb modern facilities, while its cathedral, the **Aachener Dom** (www.aachen-dom.de; daily Apr–Dec 7am–7pm, Jan–Mar 7am–6pm; fee for guided tour) incorporates one of the great monuments of early medieval Europe, the wondrous octagonal chapel built by the emperor and consecrated in 805. Using bronze, stone and marble taken from Roman remains, and graced with a superb 12th-century chandelier, it is still a breathtaking space. The Gothic chancel added later contains Charlemagne's gilded shrine, and also on view is the simple marble-and-wood throne used by emperors during their coronation ceremony. The cathedral treasury is one of the most richly endowed in Europe.

In a deep and winding valley to the south of Aachen are the timber-framed and slate-roofed houses of one of western Germany's prettiest villages. **Monschau** made its living from textiles, and the **Rotes Haus** (Red House; www.monschau.de; Apr–Nov Tue–Sun guided tours at 10, 11am and 12, 2, 3 and 4pm) beautifully evokes the family life of a prosperous clothier.

Best views

There are fine views of the Rhine from the Rheinufer-promenade in Düsseldorf's city centre, but the most spectacular panorama is from the 172m (565ft) Rheinturm (Rhine Tower; Mon–Fri 10am–12am, Sat-Sun until 1am), to the south.

DÜSSELDORF

A short way down the Rhine from Cologne, and only half the size of its great competitor, the capital of North-Rhine Westphalia has an altogether different character. While Cologne was ruled by its citizenry, **Düsseldorf** ㉙ was the seat of the glittering court of the dukes of Berg. It still wears something of an aristocratic air, best exemplified in the ducal **Schloss Benrath** (www.schloss-benrath.de; Tue–Sun 11am–5pm, May–Sept also Sat–Sun 10am–6pm),

There's great shopping to be done in Düsseldorf

a lovely baroque palace set in formal gardens just outside town. Contemporary city glitter is concentrated along the leafy avenue of **Königsallee** ('Kö' for short), one of Germany's most prestigious shopping thoroughfares, off which are boutique-crammed malls.

Much of the wealth produced in the Ruhr has traditionally been spent in Düsseldorf, and not just on shopping; the city's Altstadt has been called 'the longest bar in the world', and is given over almost entirely to pubs, restaurants and nightclubs. High culture is not neglected either, with galleries and museums grouped in an 'art axis' running north from the centre. In its modern building, the **Kunstsammlung Nordrhein-Westfalen** (www.kunstsammlung.de; Tue–Fri 10am–6pm, Sat–Sun 11am–6pm) is known as **K20**, indicating its devotion to art of the 20th century. Its pride is the collection of over 100 works by Paul Klee. The **Museum Kunst Palast** (www.smkp.de; Tue–Sun 11am–6pm, Thu until 9pm) has German works dating from medieval times to the present, and includes a superb glass collection. Away from the art axis, in the old *Land* parliament building, and complementing K20, is **K21** (www.kunstsammlung.de; Tue–Fri 10am–6pm, Sat–Sun 11am–6pm), celebrating the art of today.

THE RUHR

Covering some 5,000 sq km (1,800 sq miles), the vast conurbation of the Ruhrgebiet (Ruhr Area) has lost most of the coal mines and steelworks which made it the industrial powerhouse of Germany, but has valiantly attempted to turn its industrial heritage into visitor attractions. Strung out along a 400km (250-mile) 'Route Industriekultur', they include Essen's **Zeche Zollverein** (Zollverein Colliery, known also as Ruhr Museum; www.ruhrmuseum. de; daily 10am–6pm), Bochum's **Deutsches Bergbau-Museum** (National Mining Museum; www.bergbaumuseum.de; Tue–Fri 8.30am–5pm, Sat–Sun 10am–5pm), and the **Eisenbahnmuseum** (Railway Museum; www.eisenbahnmuseum-bochum.de; Mar to mid-Nov Tue–Sun 10am–5pm), also in Bochum, with a large collection of rolling stock and frequent live steam action.

But the Ruhr offers much more. Far from being just a sprawling collection of industrial suburbs, it's a constellation of real cities and lesser towns, all proud of their identity and many with cultural institutions – theatres, opera houses, galleries – of the first order. **Essen** ③⓪ is a cathedral city, and the **Schatzkammer** (Treasury; www.dom-essen.de; daily 11am–5pm) of its Dom (Cathedral) is full of fabulous treasures.

Away from the centre, the city's museum complex includes the **Museum Folkwang** (www.museum-folkwang.de; Tue–Sun 10am–6pm, Thu, Fri until 8pm), which has one of the finest collections in the country of 19th- and 20th-century German art. However, Essen's most fascinating offering is the home of its most famous citizen, ironmaster and 'Cannon King', Alfred

Burg Vischering in the Münsterland

Krupp. Standing in lovely parkland overlooking the Baldeneysee reservoir, the monstrous **Villa Hügel** (www.villahuegel.de; Tue–Sun 10am–6pm) is full of mementos of the dynasty who were friends with both Kaiser and Führer, and who supplied Germany with some of its most destructive weaponry in two world wars.

MÜNSTER AND THE MÜNSTERLAND

The capital city of the old province of Westphalia, **Münster** ㉛, is a stately place, its cobbled streets lined with high-gabled town mansions, its formidable Romanesque-cum-Gothic cathedral endowed with a splendid astronomical clock, still in full working order after nearly 500 years. The treaty ending the Thirty Years' War was signed in Münster in 1648; the centrepiece of the **Rathaus** (www.stadt-muenster.de; Tue–Fri 10am–5pm, Sat–Sun 10am–4pm) is the wonderfully panelled Friedenssaal (Hall of Peace), where the ceremony took place.

The Rhine Valley, with the town of Bacharach

The flat, damp countryside around the city, the Münsterland, is studded with moated country houses and castles. Two of the loveliest, Haus Rüschhaus and Burg Hülsoff, are associated with Germany's foremost female poet, Annette von Droste-Hülsoff (1797–1848), but the finest of these *Wasserburgen* is **Burg Vischering** (www.burg-vischering.de; Tue–Sun 10am–6pm), a rambling construction built on a pair of islands and housing the **Münsterlandmuseum**.

RHINE VALLEY AND MOSEL VALLEY

Both Rhine and Mosel have become bywords for a certain kind of tourism, its emblems the smart white pleasure steamer, the robber baron's crag-top castle, and the vineyard clinging to a precipitous slope. The general revelry filling the cobbled streets and wine taverns of one pretty wine village after the other makes its contribution too.

The most glamorous stretch of the **Rhine** begins just upstream from Bonn, where the rounded hills of the **Siebengebirge** (Seven Mountains) include the Drachenfels (Dragon Rock) where heroic Siegfried is said to have slain his fire-breathing adversary.

Overlooked by the huge fortress of Ehrenbreitstein, the town of **Koblenz** ❷ stands at the confluence of the Rhine and Mosel. Having risen as the Moselle in the far-off Vosges Mountains of France, the **Mosel** enters Germany near **Trier**, the country's best-preserved Roman city, its symbol the great blackened gateway known as the Porta Nigra.

Between here and Koblenz, the river loops in great bends past vineyards which in the past have yielded some of the world's most expensive wines. High points include the picturesque villages of **Bernkastel-Kues** and **Cochem**, as well as the impossibly romantic castle of **Burg Eltz** (www.burgeltz.de; Apr–Oct daily 9.30am–5.30pm), its sheer walls rising through the treetops, its interiors still with their original furnishings.

Immediately to the south of Koblenz, the Rhine emerges from a dramatic gorge, some 60km (40 miles) long, where the narrowness, speed and depth of the river, as well as the presence of rapids, once made navigation perilous – to say nothing of the depredations of robber barons. The barons' strongholds are mostly in ruins, but it's possible to visit the most formidable of them all, **Burg Rheinfels** (mid to end Mar daily 9am–5pm, Apr–Oct until 6pm, Nov to mid-Mar Sat–Sun 11am–4pm) high above the village of St Goar. Unusual fortifications to look out for are the **Mäuseturm** (Mice Tower) and other toll-castles standing four-square in the stream.

All the riverside villages and small towns along the way hope to entice visitors off their boats, none more determinedly than roistering **Rüdesheim** at the southern end of the gorge, with one wine tavern after another lining its famous main street, the Drosselgasse. More dignified places include **Boppard**, an ancient town with remains of its Roman and medieval defences.

The one essential sight along the way, however, is the **Lorelei rock**, from which a fair-haired siren is supposed to have lured sailors to a watery grave with the seductive power of her song. Her story, and much else besides, is recounted in a modern visitor centre, the **Loreley Besucherzentrum** (www. besucherzentrum-loreley.de; Apr–Oct daily 10am–5pm).

SOUTHWEST TO THE BLACK FOREST

To the south of the dynamic urban region centred on Frankfurt, the Rhine flows through a broad valley bounded by upland massifs. This is one of the sunniest regions of Germany, where vines flourish and, in the smaller places at least, life is lived in a relaxed way. The heat of summer is balanced by the cooler climate of the uplands, among them the Black Forest, which, together with Germany's largest lake, the Bodensee, numbers among the country's favourite holiday areas. Contrasting cities include fan-shaped Karlsruhe, the world-famous old university cities of Heidelberg and Freiburg, and up-to-the-minute Stuttgart.

FRANKFURT AM MAIN

With its spectacular cluster of skyscrapers, Germany's financial capital on the River Main has earned the nickname 'Bankfurt' or even 'Mainhattan'. Astride strategic communication routes, **Frankfurt** ㉝ has always gained a good living from commerce, as well as being an important meeting place. For centuries it was here that Germany's rulers came together to elect kings and emperors, many of whom were crowned in the cathedral. In 1848, it was in the city's Paulskirche that delegates from all over Central Europe assembled in an ill-fated attempt to establish a

Frankfurt's Römerberg

united, democratic Germany. The millions who come here nowadays arrive via converging *Autobahnen*, by high-speed train or
through the huge airport, continental Europe's busiest.

As well as being the seat of the Bundesbank, the European
Central Bank and the German Stock Exchange, today's Frankfurt
is a centre of media and publishing. The *Frankfurter Allgemeine
Zeitung* is generally regarded as the country's leading daily
paper and the Frankfurt Book Fair is the world's most important
event of its kind. Nevertheless, the city retains a rustic sense of
its roots, notably with its devotion to the local drink, *Äppelwoi*,
cider made from the orchards all around, best consumed in the
taverns of the charming old quarter of Sachsenhausen, just
across the river from the sophisticated city centre.

Explorations of Frankfurt usually start at its historical core,
the cobbled square known as the **Römerberg**, meticulously
reconstructed after being reduced to rubble like most of the city

Frankfurt's spectacular cluster of skyscrapers

in World War II. Opposite a splendid group of tall timber-framed town mansions is the **Römer**, the old city hall, and here too is the 13th-century red sandstone Nikolaikirche. The **Historisches Museum** (Historical Museum; www.historisches-museum.frankfurt.de; Tue–Fri 10am–6pm, Sat–Sun 11am–7pm, Wed until 9pm) is worth visiting if only to see poignantly contrasting models of the city before and after its near total destruction. To the east, beyond the fantastic postmodern art gallery called the **Schirn** (with a good café-restaurant), stands the 13th-century **Kaiserdom** (Imperial Cathedral; www.dom-frankfurt.de; Mon–Thur 9am–8pm, Fri 1–8pm, Sat–Sun 9am–8pm; free), whose most striking feature is its tower. Until the advent of skyscrapers it was the city's tallest structure. Nearby is another assertive postmodern edifice, the **Museum für Moderne Kunst** (MMK; Modern Art Museum; www.mmk-frankfurt.de; Tue–Sun 10am–6pm, Wed until 8pm), whose emphasis is on late 20th-century European and American art.

The Museum Mile

The majority of Frankfurt's galleries and museums are grouped in the 'museum mile' stretching along the Main embankment opposite the city centre. There are institutions devoted to film, architecture, postal services, ethnography, antique sculpture and the applied arts, but most visitors head first to the **Städel Museum** (www.staedelmuseum.de; Tue–Wed, Sat–Sun 10am–6pm, Thu–Fri 10am–9pm). This is one of the country's great picture galleries, with more than 600 masterpieces of European painting from the 14th century onwards. The portrait *Goethe in the Campagna* by Tischbein is one of the gallery's evergreens; Goethe was born in Frankfurt, and many make the pilgrimage to his birthplace, the sensitively restored **Goethe-Haus** (www.goethehaus-frankfurt.de; daily 10am–6pm, Sun until 5.30pm). Another place of memory is the **Jüdisches Museum** (Jewish Museum; www.juedischesmuseum.de; Tue 10am–8pm, Wed–Sun 10am–6pm), whose displays evoke the long history of Frankfurt's Jewish community, which before the Holocaust was one of Germany's largest.

THE RHINE-MAIN AREA

Frankfurt is at the centre of a constellation of prosperous cities and towns with a population of several million, but is also within easy reach of fine countryside. To the west are the sun-soaked vineyards of the Rheingau, and to the south the forested uplands of the Odenwald. To the north are more woods and hills in the Taunus, on the edge of which stands the little spa of **Bad Homburg**. Homburg, which gave its name to a hat, was a favourite resort of Kaiser Wilhelm II, as was the much larger **Wiesbaden**, capital of the *Land* of Hessen. People still visit this elegant town to soak in the thermal waters first enjoyed by the Romans, congregating around the superb domed neo-classical edifice of the Kurhaus, now a casino.

Almost opposite Wiesbaden on the far bank of the Rhine is another capital, **Mainz** ❸❹, from where the *Land* of Rheinland-Pfalz (Rhineland Palatinate) is governed. Also founded by the Romans, Mainz has long been used to ruling. In the Middle Ages its archbishops were among the most powerful figures in Germany, and many of them lie in splendid state in the nave of the city's six-towered Romanesque **Dom** (https://mainzerdom.bistummainz.de; Mar–Oct Mon–Fri 9am–6pm, Sat 9am–4pm, Sun 12.45–3pm and 4–6.30pm, Nov–Feb Mon–Fri 9am–5pm, Sat 9am–3pm, Sun 12.45–3pm and 4–5pm; free), a great monument of red sandstone. The city's most famous son was the inventor of printing, Johannes Gutenberg, and the **Gutenberg-Museum** (www.gutenbergmuseum.de; Tue–Sat 9am–5pm, Sun 11am–5pm) does him justice.

No longer a capital of anything, but still with a fascinating heritage, the area's other sizeable town, **Darmstadt**, was until 1918 the seat of the grand dukes of Hessen-Darmstadt. Under the patronage of the last duke, a pioneering Art Nouveau artists' colony was established at **Mathildenhöhe** (Matilda's Heights). Many of the original buildings can be seen, including the extraordinary 48m (157ft) 'Wedding Tower', while the artists' work is on view in the **Museum Künstlerkolonie** (www.mathildenhoehe.info; Tue–Sun 11am–6pm), as well as in the town's principal museum, the **Hessisches Landesmuseum** (www.hlmd.de; Tue–Fri 10am–6pm, Wed until 8pm, Sat–Sun 11am–5pm).

HEIDELBERG AND AROUND

Few sights in Germany are quite as romantic as **Heidelberg** ❸❺ and its **castle**, especially when the rambling red sandstone ruin high above the town and the River Neckar is seen bathed in late-afternoon light against a background of glorious wooded hills. This image, together with *Student Prince* memories of roistering, duelling students in fraternity uniforms, brings millions of visitors

Heidelberg's romantic setting

every year to the undeniably picturesque university town, whose focal point is the cobbled Marktplatz. The square is overlooked by the Heiliggeistkirche (Church of the Holy Spirit), built from the same stone as the castle, but perhaps the most fascinating edifice is the amazingly ornate corner building called the Haus zum Ritter. Not far away is the old Studentenkarzer, the student prison where many an unruly undergraduate was locked up.

Heidelberg's *Schloss* (www.schloss-heidelberg.de; daily 8am–6pm) can be reached by steps or funicular. A wonderful conglomeration of building styles from the 13th to the 17th centuries, it houses a fascinating pharmaceutical museum as well as the truly gigantic Grosses Fass, a monster barrel filled annually with that portion of the wine harvest compulsorily delivered to the castle.

Upstream from Heidelberg, the steep-sided valley of the winding Neckar is a Rhine gorge in miniature, with vineyards, hilltop strongholds, and attractive villages and old towns.

Downstream, the river joins the Rhine at **Mannheim ㊱**, a rare example of a large, planned baroque city, with a chequerboard layout of intersecting streets uniquely identified not by names but by letters and numbers. The centrepiece of this grandiose example of town planning, the Schloss, remains, but as a forward-looking industrial city the rest of Mannheim has a modern aspect. The past is more alive at nearby **Schwetzingen**, where the **Schlossgarten** (www.schloss-schwetzingen.de; daily 9am–8pm or dusk) is one of the great gardens of Europe, a mixture of formal and romantic landscape styles, with a number of fantastical garden buildings.

On the far side of the Rhine, the towns of **Worms** and **Speyer** are dominated by their massive cathedrals, splendidly towered edifices which are among the greatest achievements of Romanesque architecture. The Imperial Diet (Assembly) met at Worms, and it was before it that Martin Luther appeared in 1521, uttering his famous words of defiance, 'Here stand I, I can do no other.' To the west, the Rhine plain gives way to the wooded heights of the Pfälzer Wald (Palatinate Forest), at whose foot runs the **Deutsche Weinstrasse** (German Wine Route). The well-signposted route passes through one delightful wine village after another, among them **Rhodt**, which has some fine stone and timber-framed vintners' houses, and **Deidesheim**, a famous centre of gastronomy.

KARLSRUHE AND STUTTGART

A relatively new town, **Karlsruhe** was laid out in the early 18th century by Karl-Wilhelm, the Margrave of Baden, in the form of a fan, with a pattern of streets radiating out from an imposing baroque schloss. The schloss is now the **Badisches Landesmuseum** (Baden Regional Museum; www.landes museum.de; Tue–Thu 10am–5pm, Fri–Sun 10am–6pm; Fri after 2pm most collections are free of charge). Its fine collections include wonderful trophies from the Turkish wars. The geometrical layout of the city can be appreciated from the top of the tower. Most of Karlsruhe's 18th-century buildings have gone, but there are some fine neo-classical structures around the central Marktplatz; at its centre is a sandstone pyramid marking Karl-Wilhelm's tomb.

Stuttgart was the capital of the kingdom of Württemberg up until 1918, and is now capital of the *Land* of Baden-Württemberg. Today's Stuttgart shows only a few signs of its regal past, being a resolutely modern city with an identity based on its scientific and technological achievements. It was in Stuttgart in 1883 that Gottlob Daimler patented the internal combustion engine, and today the city is home to Mercedes and Porsche, as well

The Porsche Museum in Stuttgart

as other manufacturing companies. The **Mercedes Museum** (www.mercedes-benz-classic.com; Tue–Sun 9am–6pm) is well worth a visit, as is the smaller establishment devoted to the products of the Porsche works. The old royal schloss is now the **Landesmuseum** (State Museum; www.landesmuseum-stuttgart. de; Tue–Sun 10am–5pm), whose star exhibit is the Württemberg crown jewels. But Stuttgart's most high-profile museums are the modern **Kunstmuseum** (www.kunstmuseum-stuttgart.de; Tue–Sun 10am–6pm, Fri until 9pm) and the **Staatsgalerie** (www. staatsgalerie.de; Tue–Sun 10am–6pm, Thu until 8pm). The former's founding stock consists of Swabian Impressionist works and the latter focuses on European and American post-war art.

BLACK FOREST

The best-known of all Germany's upland massifs, the **Black Forest** or **Schwarzwald** extends for about 160km (100 miles) southwards from Karlsruhe to the Swiss border. Its blackness is attributed to its dark forests of spruce and fir, but as well as

⊙ BLACK FOREST CUCKOO CLOCKS

That enduring symbol of the Black Forest, the cuckoo clock, has a fascinating history going back to the 17th century. This was a time of agricultural depression, and farmers used to handling wood looked for alternative ways of making a living. Clockmaking as a cottage industry soon took off and, by the 19th century, beautifully carved Black Forest clocks were being exported all over the world. It was around this time that the cuckoo made its appearance, to become a firm, if sometimes irritating, favourite. Clockmaking declined in the late 20th century, but has since revived.

The fabled Black Forest

woodland there are mountain pastures, rushing streams and crashing waterfalls, magnificent timber farmhouses and living folkways. The highest point of the Black Forest is the **Feldberg** at 1,493m (4,898ft), a flattened mountain whose summit can be easily reached from the car park. On clear days the view extends to the far-away Bernese Alps. A drive along the scenic route called the Schwarzwald-Hochstrasse is one way of getting to know the area, but the Black Forest is best explored on foot from any one of the numerous highland resorts. The most popular resort is the invariably crowded **Titisee**, beautifully sited on the lake of the same name, but there are many other places to stay. Satisfying one's natural curiosity about Black Forest cuckoo clocks – and about timepieces of all kinds – can be done at the excellent **Deutsches Uhrenmuseum** (National Clock Museum; www.deutsches-uhren-museum.de; daily Apr–Oct 9am–6pm, Nov–Mar 10am–5pm). The area's distinctive building heritage can be seen everywhere, and in concentrated form at the **Schwarzwälder Freilichtmuseum Vogtsbauernhof** (Black Forest Open-air Museum; www.vogts-bauernhof.de; Apr–Oct daily 9am–6pm, Aug until 7pm), where traditional farming techniques are also demonstrated.

The Black Forest's western edge drops abruptly to the broad plain of the Rhine. One of the best panoramas is from the 1,284m (4,213ft) high **Schauinsland** viewpoint, reached by cable car from the ancient cathedral and university city of **Freiburg**. Overlooked by the tall spire of its superb Gothic **Münster** (Minster), Freiburg is a well-preserved town, with a wealth of old buildings, museums, and places to eat and be entertained. Its relaxed lifestyle may have something to do with the vineyards clothing the lower slopes of the Black Forest and the nearby Kaiserstuhl (Emperor's Seat), an ancient volcano sticking up out of the plain. When strolling around, visitors should watch out for the town's *Bächle*, narrow water channels threading through the streets.

Freiburg is a useful gateway to the Black Forest, as is **Baden-Baden**, the queen of all spa towns. Set in a lovely wooded valley, the town's springs were discovered by the Romans, and one of the spas – with state-of-the-art buildings and facilities – is named after the Emperor Caracalla who spent time here. Baden-Baden's heyday was in the late 19th century, when it was known as the 'Summer Capital of Europe', attracting the continent's royalty and aristocracy and their hangers-on. The town has succeeded in keeping much of the allure of that golden age, with an opulent casino, immaculately maintained parks and famous horseraces.

LAKE CONSTANCE

To the east of the Black Forest there's plenty of fine countryside, albeit not quite on the same grand scale. Attractive small towns abound, too, none prettier than the medieval university city of **Tübingen**, where students punt along the river. With its medieval walls and towers intact, **Rottweil** is also worth a detour. But most visitors passing this way are heading south to the **Bodensee** (Lake Constance), the great body of water shared with Austria and Switzerland and bounded to the south by the Alps. Fed by the Rhine, the lake enjoys a balmy climate and, lined with orchards and vine-

Lake Constance, with the Alps backdrop

yards as well as fascinating towns and villages, is an ideal holiday destination, understandably busy in summer. The area's largest town, **Konstanz**, stands astride the Rhine as it flows out of the main lake, the Übersee, into the lower lake, the Untersee. The town's great moment of glory came when it hosted the Council of Konstanz in 1414–18, now chiefly remembered for the burning at the stake of the radical Czech clergyman, Jan Hus. Spared by Allied bombers because of its proximity to the Swiss border, Konstanz is a pleasure to stroll around.

The same is true of the little island city of **Lindau**, on the lake's northeastern corner. Reached by causeway from the mainland, Lindau has fine old patrician houses and a lovely harbour looking over the lake to the mountains. Other delightful old towns on this sunny, southwest-facing shore include **Meersburg** and **Überlingen**, while more workaday **Friedrichshafen** – former home of the Zeppelin company

Gemütlichkeit in a Munich beer garden

– boasts the **Zeppelinmuseum** (www.zeppelin-museum.de; May–Oct daily 9am–5pm, Nov–Apr Tue–Sun 10am–5pm), whose prize exhibit is a superb full-size recreation of the passenger deck of the ill-fated *Hindenburg* airship.

The lake's islands include tranquil **Reichenau**, with a set of remarkable Romanesque monastery churches, and ever-popular **Mainau** (www.mainau.de; daily 7am–8pm or until sunset), a paradise of subtropical luxuriance, with terraced gardens rising from the lakeshore to a baroque schloss and church.

MUNICH AND THE SOUTH

Southern Bavaria is perhaps the most glamorous part of Germany, and certainly the most popular part of the country for holidaymakers, with villages of timber houses clustering round onion-domed churches against an Alpine background of lakes, forests and high peaks. This is where 'Mad King' Ludwig II sited his impossibly romantic castles, and the visitor is frequently reminded that Bavaria was a kingdom almost within living memory. Even today, it is proud to be not just a run-of-the-mill *Land*, but *Freistaat Bayern* (the Free State of Bavaria), with a right royal capital, Munich.

MUNICH

The Bavarian metropolis combines a forward-looking, cosmopolitan character with a folksy, small-town atmosphere where people can sometimes still be seen unselfconsciously wearing *lederhosen* and *dirndl*, and swaying to the blast of an oompah band while swigging beer from a substantial *stein*. Within sight of the Alps, and with an array of world-class museums and galleries and superb parks, **München** ③⑦ (Munich) attracts not only visitors from all over the world but also would-be residents from the whole of Germany. The fortunate among them find employment in famous-name, advanced industries like Siemens or BMW, the Bavarian Motor Works (Bayerische Motoren Werke).

An old city founded in the 10th century by monks, Munich rose to prominence when the Wittelsbach dynasty made it the capital of Bavaria in the early 16th century. Much of the city's present regal character can be attributed to them, particularly to King Ludwig I, whose rule lasted from 1825 to 1848. Less famous than a later Ludwig, the 'Mad King', this enlightened monarch was a generous patron of the arts, a founder of museums and galleries, and an ambitious town planner. The last Wittelsbach, Ludwig III, left his ancestors' palatial Residenz in the heart of the city as Marxist revolution broke out in November 1918.

A few years later, in 1923, it was in Munich that Adolf Hitler instigated the failed 'Beer Hall Putsch', and his Nazis always considered the city to be the 'capital of the movement'. Badly battered in World War II, Munich rose from the ashes and then

The towers of the Frauenkirche

used the 1972 Olympics to modernise further, with exemplary public transport, the pedestrianisation of the city centre, and the creation of the Olympiapark.

Around Marienplatz

Sooner or later all visitors to Munich find themselves in **Marienplatz Ⓐ**, the spacious square at the centre of the Altstadt. It is named after the gilded statue of the Virgin Mary atop a column, placed there in 1638 in thanks for the safe deliverance of the city in the Thirty Years' War. The north side of the square is occupied by the exuberant mock-Gothic **Neues Rathaus** (New City Hall), which has a glockenspiel that plays at 11am, noon and Mar–Oct also at 5pm. The authentically Gothic **Altes Rathaus** (Old City Hall) to the east now houses a toy museum. There's a fine view from the tower of the new city hall, reached by lift, and another from the tower of the nearby **Peterskirche** (St Peter's Church), reached by 300-plus steps.

In the network of streets between Marienplatz and the Residenz is the **Hofbräuhaus Ⓑ**. Established by ducal decree in the 16th century to supply the court, the 'Court Brewery' is a favourite with visitors from abroad, though there are usually plenty of locals here too, downing beer to the sound of the brass band.

From Marienplatz, Munich's main traffic-free artery, the Kaufingerstrasse (later called Neuhauserstrasse), runs westwards towards the Karlstor, one of the surviving city gateways. Over the rooftops to the north can be glimpsed the twin towers and onion domes of Munich's brick-built cathedral, the Gothic **Frauenkirche** (Church of Our Lady), with its simple but wonderfully spacious interior. In the crypt are the tombs of the Wittelsbachs.

Marienplatz was once the site of the city market, but this outgrew its original location long ago and moved to the **Viktualienmarkt**, a lively place with an amazing array of fruit and vegetables. The best places to delve into the city's history are in the nearby **Münchner Stadtmuseum** (Munich City Museum; www.stadtmuseum-online.de; Tue–Sun 10am–6pm; popular café daily 10am–midnight), which also features musical instruments and puppetry, and opposite at the new **Jüdisches Museum** (Jewish Museum; www.juedisches-museum-muenchen.de; Tue–Sun 10am–6pm).

⊘ OKTOBERFEST

Beer is more than drinkable all over Germany, nowhere more so than in Bavaria and in its capital Munich, home of the archetypal beer hall and of one of Europe's great popular festivals, the Oktoberfest. A fortnight's orgy of eating and drinking, this has its origin in the celebrations accompanying the wedding of King Ludwig I to Princess Theresa in 1810. These took place on the great meadow subsequently named after her, the Theresienwiese, the scene of today's festivities, where enormous tents are erected to shelter the countless revellers and the brass bands entertaining them. The raucous jollity is not to everyone's taste, but no one should miss the huge and colourful procession that winds its way through the city on the day the Oktoberfest begins.

The Antiquarium inside the Residenz

Residenz and Englischer Garten

Over the centuries, the rulers of Bavaria transformed what had been a simple moated medieval castle into a sumptuous palace laid out around seven courtyards. The **Residenz** ⓒ is one of the great treasure houses of Europe, reflecting Wittelsbach wealth, the family's taste as passionate collectors, and their ability to employ the best talents of the time. Too extensive to take in at one go, the state rooms of what is now the Munich **Residenzmuseum** (www.residenz-muenchen.de; daily Apr to mid-Oct 9am–6pm, mid-Oct to Mar 10am–5pm) can only be seen in their entirety in the course of two guided tours. As well as living quarters reflecting the personal preferences of successive rulers, there are stunning set pieces like the rococo Ahnengalerie (Ancestral Gallery) with its portraits of Wittelsbach ancestors, the Renaissance Antiquarium, built to house a collection of antique sculpture and decorated with murals of Bavarian scenes, and the Kaisersaal (Imperial Hall), a sumptuous setting for state occasions. One part of the complex not to be missed is the **Cuvilliés-Theater** (Apr–July, early Sept to mid-Oct Mon–Sat 2–6pm, Sun 9am–6pm, Aug–early Sept daily 9am–6pm, mid-Oct to Apr Mon–Sat 2–6pm, Sun 10am–5pm), a jewel-like baroque auditorium. Another is the **Schatzkammer** (Treasury; daily Apr to mid-Oct 9am–6pm, mid-Oct to Mar 10am–5pm), with superb examples of workmanship in gold, silver and precious stones from around AD1000 to the 19th century.

Part of the Residenz fronts on to Odeonsplatz, dominated by the mustard-yellow **Theatinerkirche**, one of the city's finest examples of baroque church architecture, and by the Italian-style loggia known as the **Feldherrnhalle** (Commanders' Hall). Built in 1844 to celebrate the achievements of the Bavarian army, the hall was the focal point of Hitler's abortive putsch of 1923, and subsequently became a place of Nazi pilgrimage. North of here stretches Ludwigstrasse, named after Ludwig I, the monarch responsible for the elegant architectural character of much of this part of the city. The broad roadway leads to the university and the vibrant Schwabing district, and terminates at

A game of volleyball in the English Garden

Theatre

The ornate Cuvilliés-Theater was built in the mid-18th century by François Cuvilliés, court dwarf and gifted designer. It saw the premiere in 1781 of Mozart's opera *Idomeneo*.

the triumphal arch of the **Siegestor**. The popularity of this part of Munich is partly due to the proximity of the **Englischer Garten D**, one of the largest public parks in the world. Extending 3km (2 miles) north from the formal Hofgarten (Court Garden) attached to the Residenz, and threaded by rushing sub-Alpine streams, the English Garden has a wealth of features including a Japanese garden, a rotunda with a lovely view of the city skyline, a Chinese tower with a 7,000-seater beer garden, and sweeping lawns for all kinds of activity and inactivity (such as nude sunbathing).

The Museum Quarter

The district to the west of Ludwigstrasse is one of the world's largest and most richly endowed concentrations of art museums and galleries. The initial impulse was given by Ludwig I, when he ordered the construction of a group of neo-classical edifices around the spacious **Königsplatz E**. They include the **Glyptothek** (www.antike-am-koenigsplatz.mwn.de; Tue–Sun 10am–5pm, Wed until 8pm), which houses a superlative collection of Greek and Roman sculpture; the **Antikensammlungen** (State Collections of Antiquities; same times), an equally magnificent array of bronzes, vases, ceramics and jewellery; and the **Propyläen**, an imposing copy of the gateway guarding the approach to the Acropolis in Athens.

Here too is the **Städtische Galerie im Lenbachhaus** (City Gallery in the Lenbach House; www.lenbachhaus.de; Tue 10am–8pm, Wed–Sun 10am–6pm), an Italianate villa with a garden to match. Once the home of the portraitist Franz von Lenbach, the gallery is devoted to Munich painting from the 18th century onwards, with particular emphasis on the vibrant, colourful work of the early 20th-century Blaue Reiter group of artists led by Wassily Kandinsky.

But the centre of gravity of the museum area is formed by the trio of prestigious *Pinakotheken* (picture galleries), just to the north. In its 19th-century Venetian-style palace, the **Alte Pinakothek** (Old Picture Gallery; www.pinakothek.de; Tue 10am–8pm, Wed–Sun 10am–6pm; cheaper on Sun) is one of the world's finest galleries of European art from the Middle Ages to the 18th century, based on the collections assembled by the Wittelsbachs. Comprehensive in scope, it has works by most of the Old Masters, with a natural emphasis on the German greats like Dürer, Cranach, Grünewald and Altdorfer, whose stunning *Battle of Alexander* of 1529 is one of the most vivid battle scenes of all time.

The **Neue Pinakothek** (New Picture Gallery; www. pinakothek.de; Wed 10am–8pm, Thu–Mon 10am–6pm; cheaper on Sun) is housed in an impressive postmodern edifice (built 1981) nicknamed the Palazzo Branca after its architect Alexander von Branca. Its theme is European painting and sculpture between

Albrecht Dürer's Self-portrait with a Fur Coat, Alte Pinakothek

the 18th and early 20th centuries. Again, German art features strongly, with fine pictures by Romantic artists like Caspar David Friedrich, amusing 19th-century genre scenes by Carl Spitzweg, and works by Impressionists such as Lovis Corinth and Max Liebermann.

The third of the *Pinakotheken,* the **Pinakothek der Moderne** (Modern Picture Gallery; www.pinakothek.de; Tue–Sun 10am–6pm, Wed until 8pm; cheaper on Sun), contains four galleries. The Bavarian State Gallery of Modern Art has a superb collection of 20th- and 21st-century work, ranging from German Expressionism and European Surrealism to American Abstract Expressionism and Pop Art. A whole room is devoted to Picasso. The Neue Sammlung presents what is claimed to be one of the most comprehensive collections of design objects anywhere, ranging from car design to computers. The Graphische Sammlung has more than 400,000 drawings and prints.

Next to the Pinakothek der Moderne is the Museum Brandhorst (http://museum-brandhorst.de; Tue–Sun 10am–6pm, Thu until 8pm), which opened in 2009. Its collection of more than 700 pieces of modern art includes works by Andy Warhol, Joseph Beuys, Eric Fischl, Alex Katz and Joan Miró.

Deutsches Museum

The largest of Munich's museums is not in the museum quarter but on its own island in the River Isar. The **Deutsches Museum ⑤** (www.deutsches-museum.de; daily 9am–5pm) is one of the world's leading museums of science and technology and Germany's most popular attraction of its kind. In dozens of sections spread over six floors there are countless exhibits inviting interactive experiences, and compelling live demonstrations. The fascinating collections include historic aircraft, locomotives, boats and road vehicles.

Olympiapark

Few Olympic host cities have built on so lavish a scale as Munich did in 1972, when an old airfield in the northern part of the city was transformed into **Olympiapark** Ⓖ (www.olympiapark.de), a world-class set of sports facilities. The park features a range of subtly contoured artificial hills, while the 290m (950ft) **Olympiaturm** (Olympia Tower) offers incomparable views over Munich towards the Alps. Very much in use today, the great event hall, the **stadium** and the **swimming pool** are still covered by an innovative tent-like roof structure. Opposite the Olympic sports facilities, the extravagant **BMW Welt** (www.bmw-welt.com; daily 9am–6pm) and **BMW Museum** (www.bmw-museum.com; daily 10am–6pm) are the great attractions for all car lovers.

Pinakothek der Moderne

Munich built an equally innovative edifice to host some of the events of the 2006 football World Cup. Nicknamed the UFO, the 60,000-seater **Allianz-Arena** (www.allianz-arena.de) on the northern outskirts is clad in a spectacular translucent skin with the startling ability to glow in three different colours: white, red and blue.

Nymphenburg

On Munich's western outskirts, the Wittelsbach's sumptuous baroque summer palace, **Schloss Nymphenburg** Ⓗ (www.schloss-nymphenburg.de; daily Apr to mid-Oct 9am–6pm, mid-Oct to Mar 10am–4pm), was begun in the mid-17th century and largely completed in the mid-18th. Its most splendid interior is the Steinerner Saal, while in the south wing is Ludwig I's

Olympiapark

Schönheitsgalerie (Gallery of Beauties), his famous collection of female portraits. The palace stables house an array of fabulously ornate royal coaches and sleighs, while the floor above is devoted to the products of the renowned Nymphenburg porcelain factory. The vast park (open until sunset) is a wonderful fusion of French and English landscape styles, with pavilions rivalling the palace in their elaborate decor.

NEUSCHWANSTEIN AND OTHER ROYAL CASTLES

The fantastical castles and palaces built by King Ludwig II may have bankrupted his kingdom, but they proved to be a wise long-term investment, having become some of Germany's most visited tourist attractions. Foremost among them is the almost impossibly romantic **Schloss Neuschwanstein** (www.neuschwanstein.de; daily Apr to mid-Oct 9am–6pm, mid-Oct to Mar 10am–4pm; timed tours), perched high up on a crag above a gorge. Begun in 1869, it's a vision of what the Middle Ages might have been, and was inspired by Ludwig's musical mentor, Richard Wagner (its interiors are filled with references to Wagner's operas). Some of the castle's interiors, like the Minstrel's Hall and the Throne Room, are decorated with the utmost extravagance, but the castle was never completed, and the unfortunate Ludwig spent little time here. The best view of Schloss Neuschwanstein in its wild setting is from the little bridge high above, the **Marienbrücke**.

At the foot of Neuschwanstein is the much older **Schloss Hohenschwangau** (www.neuschwanstein.de; same times as Neuschwanstein), a Wittelsbach summer residence where Ludwig spent a happy childhood.

Set deep among the Ammergebirge Alps to the east of Neuschwanstein, **Schloss Linderhof** (http://schlosslinderhof.de; daily Apr to mid-Oct 9am–6pm, mid-Oct to Mar 10am–4.30pm) is perhaps the most appealing of Ludwig's creations, an elegant white villa standing on the mountainside among lovely terraced gardens.

The 'mad king's' most expensive project was built on an island in Bavaria's biggest lake, Chiemsee, to the southeast of Munich. **Schloss Herrenchiemsee** (www.herrenchiemsee.de; daily Apr–Oct 9am–6pm, Nov–Mar 9.40am–4.15pm) was modelled on Versailles, even including a 100m (328ft)

Neuschwanstein Castle

Hall of Mirrors, but like Neuschwanstein was left unfinished.

GARMISCH-PARTENKIRCHEN

Germany's glamorous winter sports centre at the foot of the country's highest peak, the **Zugspitze** (2,962m/9,718ft), is also much in vogue for summer holidays, with endless opportunities for walkers and climbers in the glorious country all around. Partenkirchen is the older of the two merged towns, its main street lined with colourfully painted houses. Garmisch has a picturesque old quarter too, but its centre is more characterised by sophisticated shops and boutiques. From here it is easy to get to **Oberammergau** ㊳, renowned not only for its Passion Play, staged every 10 years, but also for its incredibly skilled woodcarvers and for the art of *Lüftlmalerei*, the ʻpaintings in the airʼ (frescoes) that adorn many of the houses. It's also easy to ascend the Zugspitze, by cable car or rack railway. A clear day attracts a capacity crowd to gaze in awe at the amazing views over much of the Alps as far as 200km (125 miles) away.

BERCHTESGADEN

Once a favourite summer retreat of the Bavarian royal family, the delightful small town of **Berchtesgaden** and its surroundings encapsulate all the attractions of the Bavarian

Alps. Painted houses, a little royal palace and wonderful views contribute to the allure of the town, which is also the home of the **Nationalpark-Haus** (www.nationalpark-berchtesgaden. bayern.de), the interpretive centre for the national park which protects the area's sublime but vulnerable landscape. The town's ancient prosperity depended on salt, and visitors can enjoy a thrilling trip into the depths of the old salt mines, the **Salzbergwerk**. Another trip is up the mountain road to the Kehlsteinhaus, also known as the 'Eagle's Nest', Hitler's perch atop the 1,834m (6,017ft) **Kehlstein**, and now a panoramic restaurant (May–Oct). Near the foot of the mountain is the **Dokumentation Obersalzberg** (www.obersalzberg.de; Apr–Oct daily 9am–5pm, Nov–Mar Tue–Sun 10am–3pm), an information centre documenting the area's Third Reich connections. But the essential excursion hereabouts is aboard one of the boats on the crystal-clear waters of the **Königsee**, giving views of Germany's second-highest mountain, the Watzmann (2,713m/8,900ft), and tying up along the much-photographed onion-domed church of St Bartholomä.

⊙ 'MAD KING' LUDWIG II

Prince Otto Ludwig Friedrich Wilhelm ascended the Bavarian throne in 1864. It soon became evident that he preferred fantasy to reality, turning away from state duties to live in a world inspired by Wagner's operas and indulge in a fascination with the extravagant culture of 18th-century France. In 1886, with his ever more ambitious building projects draining the state coffers, he was deposed and declared insane. Within days, together with his personal psychiatrist, he was found drowned in the Starnberger See, a lake south of Munich.

Königsee, St Bartholomä and the
east face of the Watzmann

AUGSBURG AND ULM

Two small cities to the west of Munich reward exploration. Founded in 15BC and named after Emperor Augustus,
Augsburg, 80km (50 miles) from Munich, had its heyday in
the late Middle Ages, when the Fugger family made it Central
Europe's banking centre. Their **Fuggerei**, a gated complex of
old people's homes, was the first of its kind in the world, and
is still home to deserving pensioners. With streets and squares
beautified by Renaissance fountains and lined with fine patrician houses, Augsburg is a stately city, its pride and wealth on
ostentatious display in the Golden Hall of the Rathaus and in
the sumptuous furnishings and fittings of the cathedral.

Ulm lies just over the Bavarian border in the *Land* of Baden-
Württemberg, 80km (50 miles) west of Augsburg. The city's
pride is its **Münster** (Minster), which boasts the world's tallest spire (161m/525ft), as well as an array of superb artworks

in its interior. Ulm's grand Gothic and Renaissance Rathaus contrasts with the tumbledown buildings of the picturesque riverside **Fischerviertel** (Fishermen's Quarter).

LANDSHUT AND PASSAU

Some 75km (46 miles) northeast of Munich, the old provincial capital of **Landshut**, once the seat of a branch of the Wittelsbach family, has kept much of its medieval atmosphere, with gabled and arcaded mansions lining the main street. The town is overlooked by the ducal castle above, and by the spire of St Martin, built in brick and the tallest of its kind anywhere. This well-preserved townscape forms a fine background to the four-yearly *Landshuter Hochzeit* (www.landshuter-hochzeit.de; next in 2021), a lavish re-enactment of the wedding in 1475 of the then duke to a Polish princess.

On a tongue of land at the confluence of three rivers – the Danube, Inn and Ilz – just upstream from the frontier with Austria, **Passau** has perhaps the most distinctive setting of any German city. Keeping a watchful eye on the town from the wooded heights above is **Veste Oberhaus**, the fortress built by the city's prince-bishops, now the regional museum. Passau's pretty painted houses are arranged around the bishops' downtown Residenz, the tall-towered Rathaus and the cathedral, which contains the world's largest organ.

REGENSBURG AND AROUND

As one of the country's largest cities to have remained unscathed by war, **Regensburg** ㊴, 130km (80 miles) north of Munich, has many historical delights. Founded by the Romans to guard their frontier on the Danube, in the Middle Ages it was the biggest city in Bavaria, and has kept a wealth of ancient buildings lining the grid pattern of streets and alleyways established by the Romans. Unique in Germany are the fortified tower houses built by prosperous medieval merchant families to flaunt their wealth and status; some 30 of these extraordinary structures have survived. Another remarkable survivor is the **Steinerne Brücke** (Stone Bridge), a 15-span marvel of medieval engineering thrown across the Danube in the mid-12th century. From it there is a fine prospect of the city still looking much as it must have done in the Middle Ages; beyond the gateway and clock tower guarding the bridge approach rises Regensburg's **Dom** (Cathedral), the finest Gothic structure in Bavaria, begun in the 13th century and completed in the 19th with the addition of delicate openwork spires. Its sculpture of the 'Laughing Angel' is famous, as is its array of stained glass.

The city's most illustrious family was the princely dynasty of Thurn and Taxis, pioneers in the 16th century of reliable postal services. The opulent lifestyle they enjoyed is on show in the **Schloss Thurn und Taxis** (www.thurnundtaxis.de; guided tours only, mid-Mar–mid-Nov daily 10.30am–4.30pm, mid-Nov–mid-Mar Sat–Sun 10.30am, 1.30pm and 3.30pm). The tour also takes in lovely medieval cloisters.

High above the Danube a short distance downstream from Regensburg stands the gleaming white neo-Grecian temple of **Walhalla** (www.walhalla-regensburg.de; daily Apr–Oct 9am–6pm, Nov–Mar 10am–12pm, 1–4pm), built by King Ludwig I of Bavaria in 1842 to honour Germany's heroes. Its array of more than 120 busts begins with the 10th-century King Henry the Fowler, and it is still being added to; the latest to be honoured is Sophie Scholl, the Munich student executed by the Nazis for her resistance to the regime.

At **Kelheim**, some 32km (20 miles) upstream from Regensburg, another prominent 19th-century monument overlooks the confluence of the Danube and the Altmühl rivers. The circular

Regensburg's medieval Steinerne Brücke (Stone Bridge)

Befreiungshalle (Hall of Liberation) commemorates the German victory over Napoleon in 1813. Beyond Kelheim the River Danube flows through a spectacular limestone gorge, a fine location for the monastery of **Weltenburg**; its church is one of the most gloriously theatrical examples of baroque architecture in Bavaria. Limestone cliffs fringe stretches of the Altmühl valley, an area of tranquil countryside, much of it protected as a nature park. The 'capital' of the valley is the exquisite little episcopal town of **Eichstätt**, with a cathedral and pastel-coloured rococo residences.

The vast **Bayerischer Wald** (Bavarian Forest) along the border with the Czech Republic has been called 'Europe's Green Roof'. Dense conifer woodland clads much of the area, which rises to 1,456m (4,777ft) at the bleak summit of the **Grosser Arber**, reached by chairlift. Part of the forest is a designated national park, its flora and fauna expertly explained in the **Hans-Eisenmann-Haus** visitor centre near Neuschönau.

NUREMBERG AND NORTHERN BAVARIA

Only incorporated into Bavaria in relatively recent times, this part of the country seems to encapsulate much of the essence of Germany. Here are beautifully preserved or immaculately rebuilt historic cities, ranging in size from old provincial capitals like **Nuremberg** 40 and Würzburg to exquisite small towns like Rothenburg ob der Tauber, Nördlingen and Dinkelsbühl strung out along the country's most popular holiday route, the **Romantic Road**.

NUREMBERG

Lovingly rebuilt after wartime devastation, the Altstadt in **Nürnberg** (Nuremberg) conveys the atmosphere of the archetypal German medieval city, with formidable defensive walls, streets lined with red-roofed old buildings, squares presided over by great Gothic churches and fabulous fountains. Overlooking it all from rocky height is an Imperial castle. The unchallenged capital of northern Bavaria, Nuremberg is associated not just with emperors and Wagner's Mastersingers, but also with some of the grimmer aspects of Nazism, in particular the ostentatious pageantry of party rallies and the post-war trials of the leaders of the Third Reich.

The Altstadt is divided into roughly equal halves by the River Pegnitz, which is spanned by the picturesque Heilig-Geist-Spital, a 15th-century almshouse. To the south, the twin-towered **Lorenzkirche** (Church of St Lawrence) contains masterworks by the great craftsmen the city nurtured at its zenith in the 15th and early 16th centuries, as does the lovely **Frauenkirche** (Church of Our Lady) to the north. The Frauenkirche has a glockenspiel with performing automata, while the marketplace it stands in is the scene of the

Christkindlmarkt, Nuremberg's world-famous Christmas market. Here too is the 19m (62ft) Gothic **Schöner Brunnen**, the city's foremost fountain, with its astonishing array of statuary. From here, Burgstrasse leads upwards past the Sebaldskirche and Rathaus to the **Kaiserburg** (Imperial Castle; www.kaiserburg-nuernberg.de; daily Apr–Sept 9am–6pm, Oct–Mar 10am–4pm), a complex structure begun in the 12th century by Emperor Frederick Barbarossa. From the main tower there is a fine panorama over the Altstadt. Below the castle is the **Albrecht-Dürer-Haus**, the residence of Nuremberg's most famous son. Some of the artist's finest work can be seen in the enormous **Germanisches Nationalmuseum** (www.gnm.de; Tue–Sun 10am–6pm, Wed until 9pm), whose huge collection of artefacts spans German culture from the earliest time.

Picturesque Nuremberg

Just beyond the city walls, the **DB Museum** (German Railways Museum; www.dbmuseum.de; Tue–Fri 9am–5pm, Sat–Sun 10am–6pm) is the largest of its kind in Germany, with a fine collection of railway artefacts and a huge model railway. Southeast of the centre, some of the monster structures erected for the Nazi Party rallies still stand, notably the incomplete congress centre modelled on Rome's Colosseum. Part of it now houses a documentation centre chronicling the Third Reich and Nuremberg's role in it.

FRANCONIA

To the north of Nuremberg, **Fränkische Schweiz** (Franconian Switzerland) is a limestone plateau cut by deep, wooded valleys. The principal town, **Bayreuth**, dates to the 12th century, but its worldwide fame is a relatively modern phenomenon, thanks to the annual opera festival celebrating Richard Wagner and his works. Bayreuth's operatic tradition had begun in the 18th century with the building of a splendid baroque opera house, one of the finest to have survived.

The Bamberger Reiter

The great jewel of Franconia, however, is perfectly preserved **Bamberg** ⊕, divided into the lower citizens' town astride the River Regnitz and the upper bishops' town. The symbol of the former is the extravagantly picturesque, medieval-cum-baroque **Altes Rathaus** (Old Town Hall), perched on an island in the river, the symbol of the latter the glorious four-towered **Dom** (Cathedral), a wonderfully harmonious edifice built as the Romanesque style morphed into Gothic. As well as the splendid tomb of Emperor Heinrich II, it contains the enigmatic mounted sculpture known as the Bamberger Reiter (Bamberg Rider), for long considered to represent the very essence of medieval chivalry, though his identity remains unknown.

Ornate churches

The lovely valley of the River Main to the north of Bamberg is flanked by two of Germany's finest 18th-century churches: Kloster Banz to the west, Vierzehnheiligen to the east. Drawing pilgrims in their thousands, Vierzehnheiligen (Church of the Fourteen Saints; www.vierzehnheiligen.de; daily May–Sept 6.30am–8pm, Oct–Apr 7.30am–5pm; donation requested) was built in the most extravagant rococo style imaginable at the site of a humble shepherd's vision.

Almost on the border with Thuringia, **Coburg** is overlooked from a great height by the old fortress known as the 'Crown of Franconia'. Through judicious intermarriage, the ducal rulers of Coburg spread their genes throughout royal Europe; Queen Victoria's husband, Prince Albert, was born here, and the widowed monarch visited Coburg several times after her consort's death, no doubt reassured by the English Tudor appearance of the ducal schloss. Albert and Victoria were first cousins.

WÜRZBURG AND THE ROMANTIC ROAD

Among the gesticulating baroque statues gracing the ancient bridge over the River Main at the university city of **Würzburg** 42 is one of St Kilian, an Irish missionary martyred here in the 7th century. A millennium or so later, the Christian ruler here, Prince-Bishop Schönborn, was living in lavish style in the magnificent **Residenz** (www.residenz-wuerzburg.de; daily Apr–Oct 9am–6pm, Nov–Mar 10am–4.30pm) built for him by the architect Balthasar Neumann. This is one of the largest and most flamboyant baroque palaces in Germany, boasting a succession of magnificent interiors and, crowning the huge staircase, the largest ceiling painting in the world, the work of the Venetian artist Tiepolo.

At the centre of the Franconian vineyards, Würzburg has a relaxed atmosphere. There's a winery in the late-medieval hospice known as the **Juliusspital**, and a tour of the wine-villages along the Main is highly recommended, as is a visit to the prince-bishops' baroque summer palace at **Veitshöchheim** (www.schloesser.bayern.de; garden: daily dawn–dusk; palace: Apr to mid-Oct Tue–Sun 9am–6pm), 7km (4 miles) from Würzburg. This is the country's most famous rococo garden, decorated by more than 200 statues.

Würzburg is the starting point of the 350km (220-mile) **Romantic Road** (*Romantische Strasse*), a signposted holiday route which leads southwards through tranquil countryside and a succession of historic towns to the foot of the Alps. The one essential stop along the way is **Rothenburg ob der Tauber ㊸**, its quaint name matching the little medieval city's perfect state of preservation. By blanking out the crowds of visitors wandering the streets, relaxing in the main square, or filing along the sentry-walk running the whole length of the 2.5km (1.5-mile) fortifications, it's easy to imagine oneself transported magically back into an idealised Germany of the Middle Ages. There's a wonderful overall view from the tall tower of the Renaissance Rathaus over Rothenburg's red-tiled rooftops to the lovely Franconian countryside. A stroll around the streets

Quintessential Romantic Road: Rothenburg ob der Tauber

reveals an almost endless succession of delightful townscapes, none more photographed than the Plönlein, a cobbled space of changing levels framed by towers and timber-framed houses. Rothenburg was spared from destruction in the Thirty Years' War when its burgomaster successfully downed a 3.25-litre (nearly 6-pint) draught of wine, a seemingly impossible feat re-created each year at the *Meistertrunk* festival.

Almost Rothenburg's equal in picturesqueness, with intact defences, superb patrician houses and a fine parish church, **Dinkelsbühl** escaped a similar fate when its children appealed en masse to a besieging general. The event is re-created at the annual *Kinderzeche* festival. **Nördlingen**, too, has kept its ramparts with their 16 towers and five gateways, and has an additional, unique attraction in the modern Rieskrater-Museum, devoted to explaining the story of the nearby 25km (16-mile) diameter crater formed by a giant meteorite 15 million years ago.

A bucolic bike ride near Neuschwanstein Castle

WHAT TO DO

With a coast, mountains, rivers and lakes, and a great variety of landscapes, Germany caters for most types of outdoor activity, and facilities are generally of excellent quality. For further information about sporting activities, see the German National Tourist Office's website www.germany-tourism.de or those of the bodies listed below (note that only some of the sites are in English).

ACTIVE PURSUITS

Hiking and cycling. Germany has a large and well-signposted network of footpaths, particularly well developed in the mountains and nature parks. Cyclists are also well catered for, both in towns and in rural areas, and it is easy to find bikes for hire. Long-distance routes for walkers and cyclists criss-cross the country; among the most popular cycling routes are those along the Rhine, Mosel and Altmühl, while the Rennsteig ridgeline path in the Thuringian Forest is justly famous. In-line skating has risen dramatically in popularity and provision is steadily increasing; for instance, a 100km (60-mile) route crosses the Fläming area south of Berlin.

For information about local hiking clubs and long-distance footpaths, contact the **Verband Deutscher Gebirgs- und Wandervereine e.V.** (National Association of Mountain and Hiking Clubs), www.wanderverband.de. Tourist information centres can provide details of local route networks, and often have free maps. **Horse riding.** Stables can be found in most holiday areas. For information, contact the **Deutsche Reiterliche Vereinigung** (National Riding Association), www.pferd-aktuell.de. You can get an overview of riding holidays at www.reiten.de.

Water recreation. Lakes, rivers and canals form an extensive network of waterways, making cruising a practicable way of exploring much of the country. The Mecklenburg lake district is particularly well suited to this sort of activity and you can take to the waters in style. Sailing enthusiasts will also enjoy the Mecklenburg lakes, as well as the broad waters of Lake Constance. The mountain areas nearly all provide opportunities for rafting, kayaking and canyoning. The breezy coasts of the North Sea and Baltic are wonderful for sailors and windsurfers, with fjords and lagoons contrasting with more open waters. For information, contact the **Deutscher Kanu-Verband** (National Canoeing Association), www.kanu. de; the **Deutscher Motoryachtverband** (National Motorboating Association), www.dmyv.de; or the **Deutscher Segler-Verband e.V.** (National Sailing Association), www.dsv.org.

Golf. Golf has enjoyed a surge in popularity in recent years, with many courses laid out in beautiful surroundings. Guest players are usually welcome. Green fees in or near large cities can be expensive, but are much cheaper in the countryside. For information, contact the **Deutscher Golf-Verband** (National Golf Association), www.golf.de.

Angling. Trout is the favourite freshwater catch, and there's some good sea fishing along the coast. For information, contact the **Deutscher Angelfischerverband** (German Fishing Association), www.dafv.de.

Climbing. The Bavarian Alps offer challenging climbing, with the possibility of staying at high altitudes in mountain huts. Rock climbers will find Germany's best rock faces in the sandstone formations of Saxon Switzerland. For information, contact the **Deutscher Alpenverein** (German Alpine Club), www. alpenverein.de.

Winter sports. Garmisch-Partenkirchen is Germany's winter sports capital, but opportunities to enjoy time in the snow

Skiing in the Alps

abound throughout the Bavarian Alps, from Berchtesgaden in the east to the Allgäu in the west. Snowfall is more limited further north, but skiers head out of the cities to upland areas like the Taunus, the Black Forest, the Harz Mountains and the Sauerland. Oberhof in the Thuringian Forest, once the GDR's prime winter resort, has particularly well-developed facilities, including a summer bobsleigh run. Information can be obtained from: www.gapa.de; www.ober-hof.de; and from the **Deutscher Skiverband** (National Ski Association), www.ski-online.de.

SPECTATOR SPORTS

Soccer. Millions of avid supporters watch the Saturday afternoon matches of the *Bundesliga*, Germany's national league, either in person or on TV. Passions reach fever pitch when the national team wins the World Cup (as in 2014) or participates in

Football mania

Westfalenstadion in Dortmund is Germany's biggest stadium, with a capacity of 80,500. It's nicknamed 'the opera house of German football' due to the melodious (and loud) chanting of the home fans.

the European Championship (last won by Germany in 1988, next chance in 2020).

Ice hockey. Although perhaps not as popular as it once was (when it came second only to football), ice hockey is still widely played throughout the country, with professional teams competing in the national league, the *Deutsche Eishockey Liga*. The season runs from September to April.

Tennis. Stars like Boris Becker, Steffi Graf and Michael Stich have helped make tennis one of Germany's most popular spectator sports. The climax of the tennis season is the German Masters championship, held annually in Hamburg.

Basketball. Like soccer, basketball has its own *Bundesliga*, in which teams compete between October and April.

Motor racing. Germany hosts not one, but two Grand Prix events every year, one at the tortuous Nürburgring in the Eifel uplands, the other at Hockenheim near Heidelberg.

Horse racing. The most prestigious meetings are the Düsseldorf Galopp – established in 1844 – and those held several times a year at the Iffezheim racecourse, near Baden-Baden.

SHOPPING

Germany has a well-earned reputation for producing high-quality manufactured goods, and a stroll around a department store will reveal any number of consumer desirables. There are also plenty of tacky souvenirs. Most German town centres have been comprehensively pedestrianised, and as a result the traffic-free shopping experience can be quite pleasant, with attractive places to sit and recover while you ponder the wisdom of your retail purchases.

As elsewhere, chain stores and department stores occupy the prime sites, while humbler establishments like antiques shops and secondhand book dealers can be found in side streets, or in particular parts of town. The *Antik und Flohmarkt* beneath the railway arches near to Berlin's Friedrichstrasse is a treasure trove of antiques. Modern shopping arcades – *Passagen* – are often very inviting, especially in the biggest cities; Berlin has state-of-the-art examples in Friedrichstrasse, and there are other fine ones in Hamburg and Düsseldorf. Large, no-frills supermarkets and warehouse-type establishments cluster on the edges of towns, usually close to an *Autobahn* interchange, and they frequently offer very good value for everyday purchases.

Markets are great for people-watching as well as bargain-hunting; Munich's Viktualienmarkt is one of the city's great sights. Flea markets like the weekend one in Berlin's Charlottenburg are a great attraction, while Christmas markets, such as the ones in Nuremberg and Dresden, are full of atmosphere as well as good places for presents. Museum shops are well-stocked, often with original items unobtainable elsewhere.

Traditional Christmas market in Ettal, Bavaria

THINGS TO BUY

Antiques. The prosperous periods in German history produced many fine goods, notably during the *Jugendstil* (the local version of Art Nouveau) and Art Deco eras. Ceramics and lamps are often of a very high quality and are available at reasonable prices. Early 19th century *Biedermeier* furniture is also very desirable.

Books. City bookshops are often palatial, offering coffee and places to sit and read, as well as quite a few books in English.

Fashion. Everything is available, from designer fashions to secondhand chic. Traditional Bavarian wear can look very smart in Bavaria, but how often would you sport *Lederhosen* or a *Dirndl* at home? A loden coat, made with the sturdy, oily wool of mountain sheep, could be a better buy. Leatherwear is usually of a high quality.

Inside Dresden's Semperoper

Food and drink. Bakeries and delicatessens are of a high standard, though there are obvious problems in getting perishable items home. Visitors with a car will be tempted to load up with excellent and inexpensive beer, wine or spirits.

Porcelain. This long-established industry is still turning out fine products. Among the leading factories are Nymphenburg (in Munich), Rosenthal (in Selb), Meissen, KPM in Berlin, and Villeroy & Boch at Mettlach in the Saarland.

Souvenirs. As well as cuckoo clocks, timepieces of all kinds are made in the Black Forest. Germany is the natural habitat of the garden gnome and of the beer *Stein*.

Toys. Germans have traditionally been great toymakers, with centres of excellence in Nuremberg (mechanical toys, including the world's best model railways) and the Erzgebirge mountains in Saxony (carved items).

ENTERTAINMENT

High culture prospers in Germany, not least because of generous subsidies; cities compete with one another in terms of cultural offerings, a situation which has resulted in the country having well over 100 opera houses. But popular culture and entertainment is vibrant as well; committed ravers will find their needs satisfied, particularly in the big cities and above all in Berlin, where clubs and other venues cater for every taste. Local papers and tourist information centres provide information, and some cities publish listings magazines.

Music, opera, theatre. In the homeland of Bach, Beethoven and Brahms, every place of any size has a programme of opera and classical music concerts. Some of the venues, like Dresden's monumental Semperoper, are visitor attractions in their own right. In addition to purpose-built halls,

The beer tents are crowded at the Oktoberfest

concerts may be held in a historic church, like Bach's Thomaskirche in Leipzig. Regular concerts take place most of the year, with the summer break often being filled with a music festival. For non-German-speakers, the appeal of theatre is obviously limited, but ballet and modern dance is well developed, and English-language performances can sometimes be found. The appeal of musicals is universal, as are the lavish revues staged at venues like Berlin's Friedrichstadtpalast.

Rock, pop, jazz. The larger cities offer the biggest names, but rock, pop and jazz can be found virtually everywhere in Germany, with many open-air concerts and weekend festivals in summer.

Brass bands. Oompah bands still dominate the scene in Bavarian beer halls, at the Munich Oktoberfest and at the Karneval celebrations in the Rhineland and elsewhere.

Nightlife. Clubs and discos abound, some of the best in university cities, where there may be a popular student gathering place like the Moritzbastei in Leipzig. Sharp and witty cabaret is a German speciality.

Cinema. Movie-houses range from multiplexes to small art-house establishments. English-language films are usually dubbed into German, though one or two cinemas in larger centres will show films in the *Originalversion* ('OV'). Global marketing ensures that the latest Hollywood blockbusters are screened almost as soon as they are released in the US.

CHILDREN'S GERMANY

You only need to observe the generous provision in cities of playgrounds and other facilities for children to realise that (despite a sharply declining birth rate) children are well catered for in Germany. Traffic-free town centres and good footpath and cycle networks also help to make the urban environment relatively child-friendly. Children from countries where trams are a novelty may enjoy riding round town aboard a *Strassenbahn*. With an abundance of lakes and rivers, and mountains with chairlifts, cable cars and (at the Brocken) a steam railway, there's usually plenty to do in the German countryside, to say nothing of the seaside with all its attractions and activities.

Museums. Museums will help keep children occupied and entertained, particularly those with plenty of interactive exhibits like Munich's Deutsches Museum (see page 114), or those with huge model railways like Nuremberg's Railway Museum (see page 126). The Chocolate Museum in Cologne (see page 86) is also a sure winner. Many museums have special programmes for children, though some German is usually required.

Zoos. There are several world-class zoos in Germany, among them Hellabrunn in Munich, Hagenbeck in Hamburg and Berlin's Zoological Garden (see page 37). The Zoo am Meer in Bremerhaven (see page 52) focuses on sea creatures and animals from the Arctic.

Theme parks. Germany's largest theme park is Europa-Park (www.europapark.de; daily Easter–Oct 9am–6pm, Dec–early Jan 11am–7pm) near Freiburg, with a spectacular roller coaster, closely followed by the likes of Phantasialand (see page 86) near Cologne and Belantis (daily 10am–6pm, Jul–Aug 9am–8pm) outside Leipzig.

FESTIVALS

Drawing on local and regional traditions, Germany has an extraordinary range of popular festivals. Many are based on the church calendar, others on historical events, which may be lavishly re-created like the July *Kinderzeche* in Dinkelsbühl (see page 129). Among the best known are the Oktoberfest in Munich (see page 109) and Karneval in the Rhineland (see page 109), but there are other events throughout the country during the course of the year. *Schützenfeste* – originally marksmen's festivals – are held in many places, with the largest taking place in Hanover in July. Music festivals tend to be in the summer months: among the most popular are those celebrating Beethoven in Bonn (Sept–Oct) and Wagner in Bayreuth (July–Aug). Some of the most spectacular events are only put on at infrequent intervals, like the Landshut Wedding (every four years – next in 2021) and the Oberammergau Passion Play (every 10 years – next in 2020).

CALENDAR OF EVENTS

February: *Internationale Filmfestspiele Berlin*: Berlin International Film Festival. *Karneval*: Cologne stages the most spectacular pre-Lenten carnival, closely followed by those of Mainz and Düsseldorf; in the south the event is known as *Fasching*; in the southwest as *Fasnet*, in which people wear grotesque masks – Rottweil is the most important centre.

February/March: Kurt Weill festival in Dessau.

Easter: Easter processions and Easter egg decoration in the Sorb areas of eastern Germany.

April: Devilish revelry on *Walpurgisnacht* (30 April) in the Harz Mountains.

Mid-May: Start of Sunday costume plays (they run until mid-September) in Hamelin celebrating the *Rattenfänger* (Ratcatcher).

May/June: Re-creation of the *Meistertrunk* in Rothenburg ob der Tauber on Whitsun weekend.

June: *Kieler Woche*: Kiel Week sailing regatta.

July: Ulm *Schwörmontag* river pageant. Heidelberg castle illuminations and fireworks display (also in June and September). Wagner festival in Bayreuth (25 July to 28 August). *Kinderzeche* in Dinkelsbühl. Rhine in Flames illuminations and fireworks in Bingen/Rüdesheim. Munich Opera Festival.

August: Hanover *Maschseefest* two-week lake festival of music and spectacles (begins late July). Hamburg DOM Festival, one of the largest funfairs in Germany (also held in March/April and November). Rhine in Flames illuminations and fireworks in Koblenz. Furth-im-Wald *Drachenstich* (Stabbing the Dragon) pageant. *Gäubodenvolksfest* beer festival in Straubing.

September/October: Rhine in Flames illuminations and fireworks in St Goar. Wine festivals throughout Germany. Beethoven festival in Bonn. *Berliner Festspiele*: A major international festival of opera, theatre, dance, music and art held in Berlin. Berlin Marathon begins and ends at the Brandenburg Gate. Oktoberfest beer festival in Munich, lasting 16 days up to the first Sunday in October; don't miss the colourful opening procession (see page 109).

December: Christmas markets in Nuremberg and elsewhere.

EATING OUT

Traditional German cuisine is unfussy, prepared from a limited range of good ingredients, with an emphasis on nourishing soups, and quantities of meat, potatoes, dumplings and various kinds of cabbage. It is satisfying, if unsubtle. More recently, *Neue deutsche Küche* – new German cooking – has extended the range, lightened the preparation and reduced amounts. In addition, foreign cuisines have been enthusiastically adopted, making eating out in Germany an enjoyable, varied and often inexpensive experience.

To accompany the meal, there is, of course, beer, Germany being one of the world's great brewing nations. The country's numerous breweries turn out distinctive products, often with a strongly regional character. But this is also a wine country, producing mainly white wines, but with a number of palatable reds, as well as *Sekt*, the local equivalent of champagne.

WHEN TO EAT

Breakfast *(Frühstück)* can be quite substantial, with cereal, protein in the form of soft- or hard-boiled eggs, cheeses and slices of cold meat or sausage, various kinds of bread ranging from chewy pumpernickel to crisp white rolls, yoghurt or *Quark* (cottage cheese), and fruit. There will normally be coffee to drink, though tea and fruit juices will also be available. Many Germans rise early and lunch late, so a *zweites Frühstück* – a second breakfast – is sometimes indulged in to fill the mid-morning gap, consisting of a filled roll or something similar.

Lunch *(Mittagessen)* is traditionally the main meal of the day, and consists of soup, a main course (often with a salad) and dessert. Classic main dishes are often pork-based, with

A typical German breakfast

Schnitzel – a thin slice of meat coated in breadcrumbs – featuring prominently. The ubiquitous potato is treated in various ways, the tastiest being pan-fried *Bratkartoffeln*, sometimes accompanied by onions and fatty bacon cubes. The favourite vegetable is *Kraut* – cabbage – in the form of *Sauerkraut* or perhaps *Rotkohl* – red cabbage. Dessert could consist of *Quark* with some sort of fruit compote or ice cream. Busy people are tending to cut back on lavish lunches in favour of lighter midday meals, leaving more ambitious eating to the evening.

Dinner *(Abendessen or Abendbrot)* is for many people a relatively light and modest meal, with much use made of bread, accompanied by cheese, cold cuts, potato salad and various condiments such as pickled gherkins. Nowadays there is a tendency to make dinner the main meal of the day, with several courses and more lavish helpings.

WHAT TO EAT

German Specialities

Brot. Germany has successfully resisted the spread of taste-less white sliced bread, and the products of German bakeries are one of the country's glories. There are any number of different types of bread, but the commonest is *Landbrot*, usually made from rye and wholemeal flour, rather grey in colour, but aromatic and with a full taste. Wholegrain *Vollkornbrot* is heavier and darker and even better-tasting, while *Pumpernickel* is denser and darker still. The best white bread comes in the form of rolls, called *Brötchen* or *Semmeln* in Bavaria.

Fisch. Ocean fish are readily available, but perhaps the most characteristic fish dishes are those made from freshwater species, among them *Forelle* (trout) and *Zander*, a larger, and to most palates tastier fish, usually translated as pike-perch.

Kartoffeln. Enthusiastically promoted by none other than Frederick the Great, the humble potato appears frequently and in many forms as well as the ubiquitous *Bratkartoffeln* described above. *Salzkartoffeln* are ordinary boiled potatoes, while *pommes frites* – often simply referred to as *pommes* – have gained in popularity. When mashed, potatoes are called *Kartoffelbrei* or *Püree*. Grated, mixed with onion, pressed into thin cakes and crisply fried, *Kartoffelpuffer* are almost a meal in their own right. *Kartoffelsalat*, potato salad, is a popular accompaniment to a sausage meal.

Spätzle. An alternative to potato, at least in the southwest, is pasta or noodles, which go under the name of *Spätzle*, literally 'little sparrows'.

Knödel. Another alternative to the potato to help bulk out a meal is the dumpling, called *Klösse* in northern Germany, and *Knödel* in the south. Dumplings can be made with flour, white bread or potato. *Leberknödel* are liver dumplings, the essential ingredient of *Leberknödelsuppe*, a broth-like soup.

Spargel. The *Spargelzeit*, the asparagus season, begins in May. The Germans have devised a way to grow asparagus that eliminates sunlight from reaching the stalks: once sunlight is removed the plants do not produce chlorophyll, and so are white. The spears develop a milder flavour and there is an increase in the sugar content. Asparagus is eaten with

Germans are sausage-mad

various accompaniments or simply drenched in melted butter.

Wild. Many menus feature *Wild* – wild fowl and game. *Reh* (venison), *Kaninchen* or *Hase* (rabbit or hare), *Wildschwein* (boar) and *Fasan* (pheasant) are often served in a rich sauce.

Wurst. It is impossible to exaggerate the importance of the *Wurst* – sausage – in German food culture. There are some 1,500 varieties of sausage, and a glance at the delicatessen counter of a large store such as Berlin's KaDeWe confirms that this is no exaggeration. Not merely a snack or a clever way of using parts of the animal which might otherwise be unappetising, a sausage can form the centrepiece of a meal. The more famous varieties include *Thüringer* from Thuringia, given extra piquancy by a shot of blood; *Nürnberger* from Nuremberg, a thin and particularly tasty sausage; and *Weisswurst* from Munich, a blander product based on veal. Then there are various kinds of slicing sausage, such as *Cervelat*, while German salami compares favourably with the Hungarian version. Spreading sausages include *Mettwurst*, *Teewurst* and *Leberwurst*, the latter coming in fine or coarse versions, with the best varieties bearing comparison with *foie gras*. The *Bockwurst*, known to the world as the Frankfurter, is heated in water before serving, while the more interestingly textured *Bratwurst* is grilled or fried. *Blutwurst* – black pudding – is best consumed in small quantities with salt potatoes and *Sauerkraut*. An essential accompaniment to most sausages is a generous helping of mild German mustard.

Regional Tastes

The regions of Germany, and even individual cities, are proud of their innumerable local specialities. Some have a strictly regional popularity, while others have become popular all over the country and can be obtained anywhere.

Eisbein. A boiled pork knuckle, a Berlin favourite. Seemingly impossible to tackle at one sitting, it can in fact be dealt with by removing the substantial quantities of fat. The accompanying sauerkraut helps cut through the residual grease. In Bavaria it's roasted and called *Schweinshax'n*.

Himmel und Erde. The Rhineland's 'Heaven and Earth' is a mixture of apples (which grow high up) and potatoes (from deep in the ground), usually served with frankfurters.

Kassler Rippchen. From Berlin, this is a pork chop, lightly salted, pickled in brine and then smoked.

Königsberger Klopse. Meatballs made from minced beef and pork. The recipe comes from Königsberg (Kaliningrad), once capital of the province of East Prussia, an area now divided between Poland and Russia.

Labskaus. Originally a fisherman's breakfast, this monster mixed dish from the North Sea coast consists of mashed-up salt beef or corned beef, pickled herrings, beetroot, onions and pickles, topped by a fried egg.

Leberkäse. Bavarian meat loaf made from minced cured pork, slowly baked in the oven giving it a crisp crust.

Leipziger Allerlei. 'Leipzig Hotchpotch' is an appetisingly colourful mixture of young vegetables, eaten as a snack on its own or as an accompaniment to a portion of meat.

Maultaschen. The German equivalent of ravioli but much bigger, this Swabian speciality consists of little parcels of pasta stuffed with a mixture of minced pork and veal.

Sauerbraten. From the Rhineland, this consists of pot-roasted beef slices in a marinade featuring redcurrant jam, cream and onions among other ingredients.

Saumagen. From the Rheinland-Pfalz, 'sow's belly' is much nicer than it sounds, a delicious meat loaf of minced, spiced pork presented in slices.

Zwiebelkuchen. Traditional flan made with onions and diced bacon, and served with new wine, from Hessen and Baden-Württemberg.

Kasspatzen, a traditional Bavarian dish of dough dumplings with melted cheeses and fried onions

Desserts

Given the substantial character of most meals, sweet things tend to be relegated to the afternoon cup of coffee, and a meal might simply be finished off with a piece of fruit or fruit compote. However, there are several types of pudding which are more or less unique to Germany. In the south, *Mehlspeisen* – desserts made from flour, eggs, sugar and milk – include steamed dumplings brushed with cinnamon or poppy seeds and *Krapfen*, a kind of doughnut. In the north, *Rote Grütze* consists of a compote of red fruits like redcurrants, strawberries, raspberries and cherries, mixed with sago or tapioca and served with cream, ice cream or vanilla sauce.

Some of the best bakery products only appear in the run-up to Christmas, among them the famous Nuremberg *Lebkuchen* – discs of glazed gingerbread – and the Dresden fruit loaf known as *Stollen*.

WHAT TO DRINK

Beer

German beer is still brewed according to the ancient *Reinheitsgebot*, the Purity Law of 1516 which insisted on the use of a limited number of ingredients – hops, malt, yeast, barley and water – and nothing else. Beer drinkers tend to be faithful to the product of their local brewery, though some brands, like Bitburger from Bitburg in the Eifel uplands, have a national profile as a result of intensive marketing.

Given the quality of German beers, few natives see any reason for drinking imported beers, though exotica like Guinness have their adherents when there is no local equivalent.

Seasonal beers

In some places, beer is brewed according to the season. Munich produces *Märzenbier* ('March beer'), while Berlin's tingling summer drink is *Berliner Weisse*, a pale beer with a shot of concentrated fruit juice.

Most German beers are of the Pilsner type: pale, bottom-fermented brews with a sharp, hoppy taste. Lighter beers with a milder taste are called *Helles*, and dark beers – *Dunkles* – can also be had. As elsewhere in the world, beer served on draught is often superior to the bottled product.

Munich is generally regarded as the capital of German beer, not least because of its thriving beer-hall culture. But some of the most characterful beers are those from the big breweries in the Ruhr industrial area, originally intended to slake the formidable thirst of coal miners and steel workers.

Nearby Düsseldorf takes great pride in its distinctive *Alt*, not unlike British bitter, and usually served in small glasses. With more breweries per population than anywhere else in the country and its own beer-hall traditions, Cologne offers a not dissimilar product, *Kölsch*, served in the same kind of thin glass. The little town of Einbeck between the Harz and the River Weser had no fewer than 700 breweries in the Middle Ages, and gave the world the name 'Bock' beer. Bamberg is known for the very individual taste of its *Rauchbier*, 'smoke' beer.

Prost!

Wine
The reputation of German wine has fluctuated over the years, and many drinkers have dismissed it out of hand as sweet,

Quality grapes

bland or character-less. This might apply to exported blended brands such as Liebfraumilch, but most German wine nowadays is at the very least drinkable, and in many cases superb.

It is worthwhile paying attention to the label before buying or ordering a bottle of wine. Ordinary wines are classified as *Tafelwein* – table wine – which can be very ordinary indeed, especially if imported wines have been blended with it. *Deutscher Tafelwein* – made exclusively from German grapes – is likely to be more palatable, with *Landwein* – country wine – being better still. Superior wines are categorised as *Qualitätswein* – quality wine, with further sub-categories indicating geographical origin or ever finer characteristics: a *Spätlese* wine, for example, is made from late-harvested grapes and is likely to have a fuller flavour, while *Eiswein* – ice wine – is the most exclusive and expensive of all, being made from grapes which have been touched by frost, yielding a wine of extraordinarily intense taste. The most widely planted variety of grape is the highly rated Riesling, followed by Müller-Thurgau. Gewürztraminer grapes are used to make a wine with an aromatic, spicy taste.

The most productive wine regions are Moselle-Saar-Ruwer, the Rhine valley, the sunny south-facing Rheingau west of Wiesbaden, Rhein-Hessen, Rheinland-Pfalz and Baden.

Interesting wines, in distinctive bulbous flask-like bottles, come from the banks of the River Main in Franconia, while eastern Germany, surprisingly, has two fascinating wine regions, a tiny one along the River Saale near Naumburg, and the larger Saxon area along the River Elbe up and downstream from Dresden.

Sparkling wine – *Sekt* – is of very variable quality. The best will be a vintage product made exclusively from grapes grown in one of the country's designated wine-growing regions.

Spirits

Schnaps is the colloquial term used to describe Germany's widely drunk, colourless, grain spirits. Among the best are juniper-flavoured *Steinhäger* in its distinctive stone bottle and *Kümmel*, flavoured with caraway seeds. A glass of schnaps goes very well with an evening meal of pumpernickel and ham. *Obstler* is a fruit brandy, with the best being made from cherries *(Kirschwasser)* and from Mirabelle plums *(Mirabellenwasser)*. Grape brandies *(Weinbrand)* range from the ultra-fiery to the velvety.

⊘ KAFFEETRINKEN

Kaffeetrinken – coffee drinking – is the equivalent of English afternoon tea, and presents an opportunity to indulge in one of the highlights of German cuisine – *Kuchen* and *Torten* – cakes and tarts or flans. Confounding foreigners' expectations of heaviness, these are made with light pastry and succulent fillings and are almost invariably fresh and delicious. The coffee is good too, full-flavoured but not bitter, going well with the little pot of cream or evaporated milk provided.

WHERE TO EAT

Traditional, inn-like eating places which welcome drinkers as well as diners are variously described in German as *Gaststätte*, *Gasthof* or *Wirtschaft*. Another type of establishment where good German food is served is the *Ratskeller*, the vaulted and often very atmospheric cellars beneath the town hall, where the mayor would not be ashamed to entertain his guests. A *Restaurant* may or may not be more refined. Restaurants serving foreign food have increased greatly in number, and in the big cities most international cuisines are represented, perhaps with more emphasis on Turkish and Balkan food than elsewhere in Europe. Most establishments have a *Tageskarte* – menu of the day – or a *Mittagsmenü* – set lunch – offering good value for two or three courses.

If it is just a snack that is required, the place to look out for is the *Imbissstube*. These booths or stands deal in such staples as a sausage served on a paper plate and accompanied by a bread roll and as much mustard as required.

An eating place may be divided into a bar close to the entrance and a dining area beyond. A large table by the bar may well be the *Stammtisch*, kept jealously for local regulars. If an establishment is busy, it is quite acceptable to share a table with other guests, though not without first asking *Ist hier frei?* Etiquette demands that fellow diners are wished *Guten Appetit!* as they start their meal, and *Auf Wiedersehen!* as they leave.

TO HELP YOU ORDER

Waiter/waitress, please! **Bedienung, bitte.**

Could I/we have a table? **Ich hätte/Wir hätten gerne einen Tisch.**

The bill, please. **Zahlen, bitte.**

I would like... **Ich möchte gerne...**

beer **Bier**
bread **Brot**
coffee **Kaffee**
dessert **Nachtisch**
fish **Fisch**
fruit **Obst**
fruit juice **Fruchtsaft**
glass **Glas**
ice cream **Eis**
meat **Fleisch**

menu **Speisekarte**
milk **Milch**
mineral water **Mineral-wasser**
potatoes **Kartoffeln**
salad **Salat**
soup **Suppe**
sugar **Zucker**
tea **Tee**
wine **Wein**

MENU READER

Aal **eel**
Apfel **apple**
Apfelsine **orange**
Backhuhn/Brathuhn **roast chicken**
Birne **pear**
Blumenkohl **cauliflower**
Bohnen **beans**
Ei/Eier **egg/eggs**
Eintopf **thick soup**
Ente **duck**
Erbsen **peas**
Erdbeeren **strawberries**
Gans **goose**
Gurke **gherkin**
Himbeeren **raspberries**
Hummer **lobster**
Kalb **veal**
Kirschen **cherries**
Knoblauch **garlic**

Lachs **salmon**
Lamm **lamb**
Leber **liver**
Linsen **lentils**
Nieren **kidneys**
Pfirsich **peach**
Pflaumen **plums**
Pilz **mushroom**
Pute/Truthahn **turkey**
Rind **beef**
Rosenkohl **Brussels sprouts**
Sahne **cream**
Schinken **ham**
Schwein **pork**
Speck **bacon**
Spinat **spinach**
Wurst **sausage**
Zunge **tongue**
Zwetschgen **plums**
Zwiebel **onion**

PLACES TO EAT

As a basic guide we have used the following symbols below to give an idea of the average price for a meal for one, excluding drinks:

€€€ over 60 euros
€€ 30–60 euros
€ below 30 euros

BERLIN AND POTSDAM
Berlin

Bieberbau €€ *Durlacher Strasse 15, tel: 030 853 2390*, www.bieberbau-berlin.de. A somewhat lighter version of traditional German cuisine. A house salad is prepared from vegetables grown in a neighbouring garden.

Hugos €€€ *Hotel InterContinental, Budapester Strasse 2, tel: 030 2602 1263*, www.hugos-restaurant.de. Much-starred restaurant atop a high-rise hotel with a view over the Tiergarten and much of the city. Mediterranean-inspired food of the very highest quality.

Leibniz-Klause €–€€ *Mommsenstrasse 57, entry from Leibnitzstrasse 46, off Kurfürstendamm, tel: 030 323 7068*, www.leibniz-klause.de. Award-winning establishment combining the functions of an above-average pub and excellent restaurant. Sophisticated German and international cuisine.

Marjellchen €–€€ *Mommsenstrasse 9, tel: 030 883 2676*, www.marjellchen-berlin.de. Filling food based on the traditional cuisine of Germany's former eastern provinces. Warm welcome and cosy atmosphere in the heart of Charlottenburg. Famous for its pig's knuckle (Eisbein), game and duck.

Ständige Vertretung € *Schiffbauerdamm 8, tel: 030 282 3965*, www.staev.de. Lively, high-ceilinged establishment on the quayside off Friedrichstrasse serves Rhineland specialities best washed down with hoppy Kölsch Cologne beer. The decor makes play with political connections.

Potsdam

Krongut Bornstedt € *Ribbeckstrasse 6/7, tel: 0331 550 650*, www.krongut-bornstedt.de. Lovingly restored group of early 19th-century buildings north of Park Sanssouci which have been adapted to house craft workshops, boutiques, cafés and a beer hall serving excellent food.

HAMBURG AND THE NORTH

Baltic Coast

Fischkopp €€ *Seestrasse 66, Seebad Bansin, tel: 038378 80 623*, www.fischkopp-bansin.de. A no-frills fish restaurant with a pleasant atmosphere and hearty portions.

Fischmarkt €€ *Strandpromenade 33, Ostseebad Binz, Rügen, tel: 038393 381 443*, www.strandhotel-binz.de. Widely held to be the best place to eat in elegant Binz, the restaurant of Strandhotel Binz serves local and international dishes, many based on its superb seafood.

Bremen

Ratskeller €–€€ *Am Markt 11, tel: 0421 321 676*, www.ratskeller-bremen.de. Enjoy north German specialities in a characterful atmosphere on the city's main square. The extent of the wine list is almost beyond belief. Also here is the far more refined, award-winning international restaurant, L'Orchidée.

Hamburg

Fischereihafen €€ *Grosse Elbstrasse 143, tel: 040 381 816*, www.fischereihafenrestaurant.de. Popular modern fish restaurant on the riverside in Altona, serving freshwater and seafood specialities. The pikeperch with home-made rémoulade is especially liked by some guests.

Old Commercial Room €€ *Englische Planke 10, tel: 040 366 319*, www.oldcommercialroom.de. Seafood restaurant by the Michaelis-Kirche with a maritime atmosphere. Try *Labskaus*, the traditional seaman's dish.

Lübeck

Haus der Schiffergesellschaft €€ *Breite Strasse 2, tel: 0451 76776*, www. schiffergesellschaft.com. You'll dine on traditional Baltic-region fare and in Hanseatic style in the 16th-century guildhouse of the town's sea captains, surrounded by model sailing ships with original banqueting tables and benches.

Wismar

Alter Schwede €€ *Am Markt 20/22, tel: 03841 283 552*, www.alter-schwede-wismar.de. On Wismar's main square, this is the Hansa town's oldest building, full of atmosphere in which to enjoy satisfying traditional food, with heavy meat sauces.

DRESDEN AND THE TWO SAXONYS
Dessau

Kornhaus €–€€ *Kornhausstrasse 146, tel: 0340 6501 9963*, www.kornhaus-dessau.de. On the banks of the Elbe on the northwestern outskirts of the city, this restaurant is one of the key buildings in Dessau's Modernist heritage (Bauhaus style). The hearty food makes much use of fresh local ingredients.

Dresden

Coselpalais €€ *An der Frauenkirche 12, tel: 0351 496 2444*, www. coselpalais-dresden.de. Central baroque palace offering refined French and German cuisine in an elegant setting. Its Grand Café is the place for superlative coffee and cakes.

Italienisches Dörfchen € *Theaterplatz 3, tel: 0351 498 160*, www.italienisches-doerfchen.de. There is solid Saxon food in the Kurfürstenzimmer, Italian cuisine in the Bellotto, and delicious cakes in the patisserie in a historic riverside setting.

Leipzig

Auerbachs Keller €–€€ *Mädlerpassage, Grimmaische Strasse 2–4, tel: 0341 216 100*, www.auerbachs-keller-leipzig.de. Atmospheric vaulted cellars and a popular place to dine in the heart of town, serving a mixture of Saxon and international dishes. The portions are quite big, some would say uninspiring, but this is a place you go to more for the experience than the food.

Stadtpfeiffer €€€ *Augustusplatz 8, tel: 0341 217 8920*, www.stadtpfeiffer. de. Set in the modern building of the Gewandhaus, home of the renowned orchestra. Impeccable gourmet food of the utmost refinement.

Meissen

Vincenz Richter € *An der Frauenkirche 12, tel: 03521 453 285*, www. vincenz-richter.de/restaurant. Charming and popular 16th-century wine tavern that is the place to come to enjoy refined versions of traditional Saxon cooking and to sample fine local wines.

WEIMAR AND THURINGIA

Eisenach

Weinrestaurant Turmschänke €€€ *Karlsplatz 28, tel: 03691 213533*, http://turmschaenke-eisenach.de. Housed in an atmospheric building from 1910 adjoining a medieval tower, this restaurant goes a sophisticated step beyond local Thuringian fare, and complements its noble qualities with a superior wine list.

Weimar

Hanz und Franz € *Erfurter Strasse 23, tel: 03643 4573 987.* An unpretentious establishment, which serves both hearty, traditional Thuringian specialities and lighter, modern dishes, including vegetarian and vegan options.

HANOVER AND THE HARZ

Göttingen

Nudelhaus € *Rotestrasse 13, tel: 0551 44 263,* www.nudelhaus-goettingen.de. Wide choice of handmade noodles and pasta served with just about everything (meat, vegetables, seafood), according to both Italian and local Lower Saxony tradition.

Hameln

Pfannekuchen € *Hummenstrasse 12, tel: 05151 41 378,* www.pfannekuchen-hameln.de. It's all about the pancakes at this cosy café-restaurant, located in one of Hameln's historic town houses. The traditional lace-trimmed décor and friendly atmosphere make this a comforting stop.

Hanover

Waldgasthaus Entenfang €–€€ *Eilersweg 1, tel: 0511 794 939,* www.entenfang-hannover.de. This cosy restaurant in the former hunting cottage of the Hanover monarchs serves fantastic regional specialities, especially wild fowl and duck. Beer garden in summer.

Lüneburg

Neptun's Fischhaus €€ *Bei der Abtspferdetränke 1, tel: 04131 408528,* www.neptuns-fischhaus.de. A friendly, family-run restaurant in the centre of town known for its good-value menu of fresh, simple fish and seafood dishes. Closed Monday.

Quedlinburg

Weinstube €–€€ *Romantik Hotel am Brühl, Billungstrasse 11, tel: 03946 96 180,* www.hotelambruehl.de/weinstube-am-bruhl. Stylish food served in the charming wine cellar of one of Quedlinburg's most attractive hotels. The cuisine is best accompanied by wines from the nearby Saale-Unstrut region.

COLOGNE, THE RUHR AND RHINE
Cologne

Heising und Adelmann €€ *Friesenstrasse 58–60, tel: 0221 130 9424,* www. heising-und-adelmann.de. Trendy establishment near Hohenzollernring serving creative international cuisine. Long bar, terrace and beer garden.

Düsseldorf

Brauerei Zum Schiffchen € *Hafenstrasse 5, tel: 0211 132 421,* www.brau-erei-zum-schiffchen.de. An Altstadt institution, the 'Little Ship' combines cheerful beer-hall atmosphere with generous portions of hearty food.

Rhine Valley

Roter Osche €€ *Hochstrasse 27, Rhens, tel: 02628 2221,* www.roter-ochse.de. The Red Ox is a German restaurant specialising in locally sourced game dishes. The portions are hearty and the atmosphere friendly – there's a beer garden too, and a little family-run hotel upstairs.

SOUTHWEST TO THE BLACK FOREST
Baden-Baden

Zum Alde Gott €€–€€€ *Weinstrasse 10, Baden-Baden-Neuweier, tel: 07223 5513,* www.zum-alde-gott.de. This award-winning establishment offers diners regional and international specialities based firmly on seasonal produce. Wild game, trout and sea bass are often on the menu.

Frankfurt

Main Tower Restaurant €€–€€€ *53rd floor, Neue Mainzer Strasse 52, tel: 069 3650 4777,* www.maintower-restaurant.de. Dine in great style on international cuisine 200m (660ft) up at the top of the skyscraper home of the Bundesbank.

Zum Gemalten Haus € *Schweizer Strasse 67, tel: 069 614 559*, www.zumgemaltenhaus.de. One of the best places to sample tasty and filling local specialities such as green sauce and spare ribs with sauerkraut.

Freiburg

Colombi Hotel €€€ *Rotteckring 16, tel: 0761 21 060.* In the heart of the Black Forest, Freiburg's leading hotel has 112 stylish rooms including an elegant suite with views of the picturesque old town. The Michelin-star Falken-und-Zirbelstube is run by chef Renee Rischmeyer.

Heidelberg

Schlossweinstube €€ *Schlosshof 1, tel: 06221 97 970.* Stylish dining in Heidelberg's Castle, where contemporary design complements the historic atmosphere. Try their perch, sorrel or venison.

Konstanz

Petershof €–€€ *St-Gebhard-Strasse 14, tel: 07531 993 399,* www.petershof.de. A homely atmosphere to enjoy fish fresh from Lake Constance and juicy roasts of meat.

Stuttgart

Weinstube Kachelofen € *Eberhardstrasse 10, tel: 0711 242 378,* www.weinstubekachelofen.de. A city-centre institution, serving traditional Swabian specialities, like strips of ham with cheese *spaetzle*, pork roast from the oven with bread dumplings, or tripe with farmhouse bread.

MUNICH AND THE SOUTH

Augsburg

Die Ecke € *Elias-Holl-Platz 2, tel: 0821 510 600,* www.restaurant-die-ecke.de. Cheerful bistro in a three-storey former craftsmen's house, behind the city's Rathaus (Town Hall), offers Swabian and Bavarian dishes.

Berchtesgaden

Bräustüberl € *Bräuhausstrasse 13, tel: 08652 976 724*, http://braeustue-berl-berchtesgaden.de. Brewery restaurant dishing up unpretentious but very satisfying Alpine food from Bavaria and nearby Austria. Goulash and pork knuckle on the menu.

Munich

Dallmayr €€–€€€ *Dienerstrasse 14–15, tel: 089 213 5100*, www.dall-mayr.com. Family-owned delicatessen that can be traced back three centuries. With an elegant restaurant serving fine food made from the freshest ingredients.

Pfistermühle €€ *Pfisterstrasse 4, tel: 089 2370 3865*, www.pfistermue-hle.de. North of Marienplatz, this restaurant serves refined Bavarian cuisine (try the ragout of deer in juniper sauce), complemented by an excellent selection of Franconian and other wines.

Schneider Bräuhaus € *Tal 7, tel: 089 290 1380*, www.schneider-brau-haus.de. An authentic Munich inn with a central location and lots of atmosphere, a mixed clientele and heaps of hearty meat-based dishes from its own slaughterhouse.

NUREMBERG AND NORTHERN BAVARIA

Nuremberg

Goldenes Posthorn € *Glöckleinsgasse 2, tel: 0911 225 153*, www.goldenes-posthorn.de. Atmospheric 500-year-old establishment in the heart of the Old Town. The succulent Franconian dishes have won countless awards.

Regensburg

Historische Wurstkuchl € *Thundorferstrasse 3, tel: 0941 466 210*, www.wurst-kuchl.de. An essential stop close to the river. The menu is sausages and more sausages – but what sausages! The sauerkraut is the real thing, too.

A–Z TRAVEL TIPS

A SUMMARY OF PRACTICAL INFORMATION

A

ACCOMMODATION (See also Camping, Youth Hostels and Recommended Hotels)

Germany offers everything from world-class luxury hotels to humble hostels. Hotel chains are well represented, many of them with familiar names, others whose operations are restricted to Germany and perhaps the neighbouring countries. Rates compare favourably with those of other European countries, and the vast majority of establishments are spotless, well-maintained and run to high professional standards.

More information about accommodation can be obtained from the Hotelverband Deutschland (www.hotellerie.de) and the German National Tourist Board (www.germany-tourism.de).

Hotels *(Hotels)* are rated by the star system (1–5), which takes account of room sizes and facilities. Breakfast is normally included in the price. A *Hotel Garni* provides breakfast but not other meals. **Guest houses or inns** *(Gasthöfe, Gästehäuser, Pensionen)* are a simpler and cheaper alternative to hotels. **Bed and breakfast** *(Fremdenzimmer)* establishments are usually comfortable and clean, provide breakfast, and are a good way to meet local people. Staying at **self-catering** *(Ferienwohnungen, Ferienappartements)* establishments helps to minimise costs. High and low seasons vary from place to place. Along the coast, the high season inevitably means summer; in the Alpine ski resorts, it'll be winter. Popular cities like Berlin, Munich and Dresden have long tourist seasons that run from spring through to autumn, though business can surge in winter for the Christmas and New Year period. Although some tourist-zone hotels do close for their low season, others go into lower-level mode and offer lower rates to compensate.

Do you have a single room/double room? **Haben Sie ein Einzelzimmer/ein Doppelzimmer?**
What does the room cost? **Was kostet das Zimmer?**

TRAVEL TIPS

AIRPORTS

Frankfurt Airport (FRA; tel: 0180 6372 4636; www.frankfurt-airport.com), 12km (7.5 miles) southwest of the city, is continental Europe's busiest airport. It has rapid connections to the centre of town by S-Bahn (Metro), train, bus and taxi. Berlin currently has two airports. **Berlin-Tegel** (TXL; tel: 30 6091 1150; www.berlin-airport.de) is 8km (5 miles) northwest of the city centre, and is connected to the city by express bus and taxi. **Berlin-Schönefeld** (SXE; tel: 30 6091 1150; www.berlin-airport.de) is 18km (11 miles) southeast of the city centre, and is connected to the city by S-Bahn (Metro), train and taxi. In 2020, Tegel is probably due to close and an expanded Schönefeld is to be renamed **Berlin-Brandenburg Airport** (BER; tel: 30 6091 1150; www.berlin-airport.de). **Munich Airport** (MUC; tel: 089 975 00; www.munich-airport.de) is 32km (20 miles) northeast of the city, and connected it to it by S-Bahn (Metro), express bus and taxi. Other cities with international airports include Cologne-Bonn, Dresden, Düsseldorf, Hamburg, Hanover, Leipzig-Halle, Nuremberg and Stuttgart.

Where can I get a taxi? **Wo finde ich ein Taxi?**
How much is it to the centre? **Wieviel kostet es ins Zentrum?**
Does this bus go to the main railway station? **Fährt dieser Bus zum Hauptbahnhof?**

B

BICYCLE HIRE

Enquire about bicycle hire at the local tourist information centre or look in the *Gelbe Seiten* (Yellow Pages) under FAHRRADVERLEIH. German railways have a bike hire service, 'Call a Bike', in Berlin, Cologne, Frankfurt, Stuttgart and Munich, and links with other providers, in Hamburg for instance (tel: 0700 0522 5522; www.callabike-interaktiv.

de). Information on cycling in Germany may be obtained from the Allge-meiner Deutscher Fahrrad-Club (National Cycle Club), www.adfc.de.

> I'd like to rent a car **Ich möchte bitte ein Auto mieten.**
> tomorrow **für morgen**
> for one day/week **für einen Tag/für eine Woche**
> Please include full insurance. **Bitte schliessen Sie eine
> Vollkaskoversicherung ab.**

BUDGETING FOR YOUR TRIP

With its high standard of living, Germany is commonly thought of as an expensive country, but with its high quality of goods and services, most visitors feel they get good value for their money.

Getting to Germany. The cost of getting to Germany from the UK and Ireland by air varies considerably. Flying with low-cost carrier Ryanair one-way can cost as little as a few pounds or euros (plus taxes and other charges), but £30–60 is probably nearer the average. Carriers such as British Airways, BMI, Virgin Express, Aer Lingus, Lufthansa and Air Berlin also offer decent rates.

Going by bus from London to Berlin, Cologne, Munich and other cities is likely to be the cheapest. By train, Eurostar from London St Pancras to Paris and Brussels, connecting with Thalys, TGV and ICE high-speed trains to Germany, offers excursion and advance-purchase tickets, as does the Channel Tunnel car-transporter.

Accommodation. Hotels (double room per night): 5-star €300–400, 4-star €200–300, 3-star €100–200, 2- and 1-star €100 or less. Similar accommodation in a *Gasthof* or *Fremdenzimmer* costs €50–70. Rates may double during a trade fair.

Meals. A decent three-course meal ordered from the *Tageskarte* could cost as little as €15, while a gourmet meal with wine at a sophisticated restaurant will cost upwards of €60.

Entertainment. Approximate prices are: cinema from €8 (reductions on some evenings), nightclub €5–20, theatre or opera €20 upwards (average around €35), amusement park adult €25, child €20.

Sightseeing. Entry to museums averages around €8, and there are reductions for children and students.

Taxis. A minimum fee of around €4 is usually charged, plus a charge per kilometre of about €1.80.

C

CAMPING

Germany has over 2,000 official campsites, graded according to the facilities offered. Sites tend to be full in the holiday season, and it is advisable to reserve a pitch in advance. The Deutscher Camping-Club (German National Camping Club) has a useful website: www.camping-club.de. Campsites range from €3 to €12 per person and €3 to €8 per tent, with extra fees for a caravan or car.

CAR HIRE (See also Driving)

To hire a car you will normally need to be over 21 and to have held a valid driving licence for at least one year. An international licence is not necessary for visitors from EU countries, Canada or the USA. Insurance is compulsory and it is prudent to take out full cover. A deposit is not necessary if you pay by credit card. A small car will cost around €50 per day, €300 per week.

Avis, tel: 069 500 700 20; www.avis.de.
Budget, tel: 69 710 445 596; www.budget.de.
Europcar, tel: 040 520 188 000; www.europcar.de.
Hertz, tel: 01805 333535; www.hertz.de.

CHILDREN

Travelling with children in Germany is fairly easy, although occasionally you may come across a hotel where youngsters are not welcome. Otherwise, Germany can be quite an interesting country for children, with lots of family-friendly museums, theme parks and festivals. Reduced entry prices for children are a standard practice, although the age limit may vary, from 12 to 18 years old. Public transport provides discounts for children under 16, while those under four travel free of charge. You can also buy adult/children group rail tickets, sometimes saving a substantial amount of money (www.bahn.com).

CLIMATE

Germany has a continental climate tempered by Atlantic influences. This gives warm, rather than extremely hot summers, and cool, rather than icy winters. Rainfall occurs throughout the year, rising somewhat in the summer months, particularly in the south. The Alps are the wettest region and also experience the most snowfall, with ski slopes generally functioning between mid-December and March. Snowfall in other upland areas is less constant. Winds are strongest on the North Sea coast, while the warm, dry wind known as the *Föhn* blowing north from the Alps can create exceptionally clear conditions as well as causing headaches and even depression among those exposed to it. The best time to come to Germany is from May to September, though city visits can be made at any time. Popular tourist areas like the Rhine gorge can get very crowded at the height of summer. Sea-water temperatures rarely rise above 18°C (64°F).

CLOTHING

The changeability of the weather means that you should pack clothes to match a variety of conditions. Even in summer, a waterproof outer garment is essential, with something warm for cool evenings. Bring a warm coat in winter.

Smart casual style will carry you through semi-formal occasions like the theatre or opera. Sturdy footwear is an asset for sightseeing, and proper walking shoes are best for mountain and forest walks.

CRIME AND SAFETY

The level of crime in Germany corresponds to the European average and visitors should take the usual precautions. These include leaving valuables in the hotel safe, being aware of pickpockets in crowded areas, and not leaving bags, cameras and similar objects unattended. Car theft is fairly common. Thieves should not be tempted by leaving items of interest on display in the car. Consider leaving the car in a guarded car park, especially overnight.

D

DISABLED TRAVELLERS

Useful sources of information and advice are:

UK: Tourism for All, c/o Vitalise, Shap Road, Kendal, LA9 6NZ, tel: 0845 124 9971; www.tourismforall.org.uk.

Germany: Bundesarbeitsgemeinschaft der Clubs Behinderter und ihrer Freunde (National Association of Clubs for the Disabled and their Friends), Elbinger Strasse 2, 60487 Frankfurt am Main, tel: 069 9705 220; www.cebeef.com.

DRIVING

To drive your own car in Germany you will need a valid driving licence, a vehicle insurance certificate, a red breakdown triangle, spare light bulbs and a first-aid kit. Non-EU citizens also need to bring the vehicle registration document.

Road conditions. The road network is maintained to a high standard, and has a comprehensive network of toll-free *Autobahnen* (motorways) identified by numbers preceded by a letter A, and *Bundesstrassen* (federal main roads) identified by a letter B. Urban roads can be severely congested during rush hours, while the Autobahn can get crowded at holiday times.

There is no general speed limit on the Autobahn, though there is an advisory limit of 130kmh (80mph). In built-up areas, indicated by a yellow place-name sign, the limit is 50kmh (31mph), elsewhere 100kmh (62mph). The use of front and rear seat belts is compulsory. Drive on the right and give way to traffic coming from the right unless on a road identified by a yellow diamond priority sign. Give way to passengers boarding or alighting at a tram stop. There are severe penalties for drinking and driving: the police may issue on-the-spot fines and may confiscate vehicles.

Are we on the right road to ... ? **Fahren wir richtig nach ... ?**
Full tank please **Volltanken bitte**
Please check the oil/tyres/battery **Bitte kontrollieren Sie
    das Öl/die Reifen/die Batterie**

Parking *(Parken)*. Parking is strictly regulated, with no parking within 5m/yds of a pedestrian crossing or road junction or within 15m/yds of a bus or tram stop. On-street parking is regulated by the standard blue P sign with times and conditions set out on a panel below. Payment is by ticket machine, parking meter or by means of a parking disc obtained from shops or petrol stations.

Breakdowns and assistance. A warning triangle must be displayed to indicate a broken-down vehicle and hazard lights must be switched on. Call ADAC (German Automobile Club) on 01802 22 22 22 (www.adac.de) for assistance. The police must be called on 110 if anyone is injured. The ambulance service and fire brigade can be reached on 112.

Road signs. You might come across some of the following:

Baustelle Works/Construction site
Einbahnstrasse One-way street
Einordnen Get into lane
Fussgänger Pedestrians
Glatteis Icy surface
Langsam fahren Drive slowly

Parkplatz Car park
Rastplatz Rest area
Stau Congestion/Queue
Tankstelle Petrol station
Umleitung Detour
Vorsicht! Take care!

E

ELECTRICITY

The standard is 230 volt, 50-cycle AC. Plugs are the continental type, and British and North American appliances need an adaptor; American 110V appliances need a transformer.

EMBASSIES AND CONSULATES

All embassies are in Berlin. Britain, the US and Canada have consulates in Düsseldorf, Hamburg, Stuttgart and Munich; Britain and Australia have consulates in Frankfurt.

Australia: Wallstrasse 76–79, 10179 Berlin, tel: 030 880 0880; www.germany.embassy.gov.au

Ireland: Jägerstrasse 51, 10117 Berlin, tel: 030 220 720; www.embassyofireland.de

New Zealand: Friedrichstrasse 60, 10117 Berlin, tel: 030 206 210; www.nzembassy.com

South Africa: Tiergartenstrasse 18, 10785 Berlin, tel: 030 220 730; www.suedafrika.org

UK: Wilhelmstrasse 70, 10117 Berlin, tel: 030 204 570; http://ukingermany.fco.gov.uk/de

EMERGENCIES

The following are the numbers for the emergency services:

Police 110, Ambulance 112, Fire 112.

> I need a doctor **Ich brauche einen Arzt**
> an ambulance **einen Krankenwagen**
> a hospital **ein Krankenhaus**

G

GETTING TO GERMANY

By air. British Airways (www.ba.com) flies from several UK airports to multiple German cities. Other airlines that fly from the UK to Germany include bmi (www.flybmi.com) and klm (www.klm.com). Ryanair (www.ryanair.com) flies from airports in Britain and Ireland. Aer Lingus (www.aerlingus.com) flies from Dublin.

By rail. The German rail network is linked to many European countries by direct trains. Eurostar (tel: 08432 186 186; www.eurostar.com) trains from London connect at Brussels with German trains using the Thalys (www.thalys.com) high-speed line to Cologne, where there are good connections to all major destinations in Germany. Luxurious sleeper trains run between Brussels and Berlin. DB (Deutsche Bahn; German Railways) has a very useful website, www.bahn.de.

By road. Germany is linked by good roads to all neighbouring countries. From Britain, the Eurotunnel Shuttle (tel: 08443 353 535; www.eurotunnel.com) and the multiple ferry services on the Dover–Calais crossing are convenient for western and southwestern Germany. Other ferries from the UK serve Esbjerg, IJmuiden, Rotterdam, Hook of Holland, Zeebrugge and Ostend. There are no direct ferry services between Britain and Germany.

By bus. Eurolines (tel: 08705 143219; www.eurolines.com) operates bus services between London and many German cities.

GUIDES AND TOURS

Details of tours may be provided in hotels, but local tourist informa-

tion centres can offer a more comprehensive view of what is available. Walking tours of cities can be a fascinating alternative to the more conventional round trip *(Stadtrundfahrt)* by buses.

H

HEALTH AND MEDICAL CARE

Germany has reciprocal health-care arrangements with other EU countries including the UK. Emergency medical treatment will normally be provided at a reduced cost or sometimes free of charge as long as you can produce a European Health Insurance Card (available from post offices in the UK and online at www.ehic.org.uk). Visitors from non-EU countries should check that their medical insurance covers them for travel in Germany, and even EU citizens should consider insuring themselves privately, for example to pay for repatriation in a medical emergency.

In case of accident or serious illness, call the ambulance service on 112. Pharmacies *(Apotheken)* are open during normal shopping hours, and when shut display the address of the nearest one open.

L

LANGUAGE

The national language of Germany is *Hochdeutsch* – High German – but distinctive regional and local dialects continue to be spoken in many areas, at least in informal settings. English is widely spoken or understood, particularly by people in the tourism and hospitality industries and by the young. The *Berlitz German Phrase Book & Dictionary* covers most of the situations you are likely to encounter in Germany.

LGBTQ TRAVELLERS

Germany is one of the more tolerant countries for LGBTQ travellers, though there are striking contrasts between what is considered acceptable behaviour. Overt behaviour is frowned upon in rural areas where strongly conservative attitudes prevail. At the other end of the spectrum, Berlin has a claim to be considered the gay capital of Europe. The 'scene' is vibrant, with numerous welcoming cafés, bars and clubs, and high-profile events like the Lesbian and Gay City Festival in late June.

M

MAPS

The local maps supplied free by tourist information centres, car-hire firms and some hotels and banks are often all you will need. The 1:200,000 scale *MaxiAtlas Deutschland*, published by ADAC (German Automobile Club) and available in the UK through the Automobile Association shows every road in the country.

MEDIA

Newspapers and magazines. The leading serious daily newspapers are the FAZ – *Frankfurter Allgemeine Zeitung* – and the *Süddeutsche Zeitung* of Munich. The popular daily *Bild* leads the field in scandal and sensation. *Der Spiegel* and *Focus* are the most authoritative weeklies. English-language publications like the *International Herald Tribune* are widely available, especially at newsstands in the larger cities.

Radio and television. The BBC World Service can be found on a number of wavelengths, and the British Forces Broadcasting Service broadcasts pop music on BFBS 1 and magazine-style content including Radio 4 and 5 Live on BFBS 2. German TV has two commercial-free national channels – ARD and ZDF – and multiple private and cable channels, while the satellite TV provided by most hotels invariably includes CNN and sometimes BBC World News.

MONEY

The euro (€) is the official currency used in Germany. Notes are denominated in 5, 10, 20, 50, 100 and 500 euros; coins in 1 and 2 euros and 1, 2, 5, 10, 20 and 50 cents.

Changing money. The easiest way to obtain euros is with a suitable debit/credit card at a cash machine (ATM; Bankomat). Foreign currency can be changed at an ordinary bank *(Bank)*, a savings bank *(Sparkasse)* or at a bureau de change *(Wechselstube)*.

Credit cards are widely accepted but not to the same extent as in the US and UK, especially in smaller establishments.

VAT (value-added tax, Umsatzsteuer or USt) can be refunded on purchases made by residents of non-EU countries when they leave the country, provided documentation has been kept.

O

OPENING TIMES

Most shops open Monday to Friday 9am and close between 6pm and 8pm; on Saturday they close between noon and 8pm. Most museums open at 9am or 10am until 5pm or 6pm, frequently later on one evening a week. Almost all are closed on Monday.

Banking hours are usually 9am to 4pm Monday to Friday, with a later opening to 6pm on one or two days a week, usually Thursday. Smaller establishments may close at lunchtime. Bureaux de change keep longer hours, and some are open 24/7.

P

POLICE

The police wear either dark blue or green and khaki uniforms and drive white motorcycles and either blue and white or green and white patrol cars. They are armed, generally courteous and efficient, if not particularly friendly. The police emergency number is 110.

Where's the nearest police station? **Wo ist die nächste Polizeiwache?**

POST OFFICES

The Deutsche Post (Federal Mail) is identified by its use of the colour yellow and its black posthorn logo. Post offices are usually open Monday to Friday 8am to 6pm and Saturday 8am to noon. Smaller offices may close earlier. For poste restante, letters should be marked *postlagernd*. If there is more than one slot in the yellow letter boxes *(Briefkasten)*, deposit non-local mail in the slot marked *Andere Postleitzahlen* or *Andere PLZ*.

PUBLIC HOLIDAYS

Banks, post offices, government offices and many other businesses close on the following national holidays. There are also many regional and local holidays, several of them connected with events in the church calendar.

1 January *Neujahr* New Year's Day
March/April *Karfreitag, Ostermontag* Good Friday, Easter Monday
1 May *Tag der Arbeit* Labour Day
May *Christi Himmelfahrt* Ascension Day
May/June *Pfingsten* Whit Monday
3 October *Tag der Deutschen Einheit* Day of German Unity
25, 26 December *Weihnachten* Christmas

T

TELEPHONES

Most telephone services are operated by the national company, Deutsche Telekom. The country code for Germany is 49. To call Germany from Britain, dial 00 49, then the area code omitting the zero, followed by the number. To call Britain from Germany, dial 00 44, followed by the local code minus the zero, then the number. For domestic enquiries, tel: 11 833; for international, tel: 11 834.

Most phone booths accept phone cards in various denominations, and some accept credit cards. Phone cards can be obtained from post offices, newspaper kiosks and petrol stations.

Most British mobile phones will work in Germany, but check charges before leaving.

TIME ZONES

Germany follows Central European Time (GMT plus 1 hour), and in summer (end Mar–end Oct) an hour is added for Daylight Saving.

New York	London	**Berlin**	Jo'burg	Sydney	Auckland
6am	11am	**noon**	1pm	10pm	midnight

TIPPING

In restaurants, a service charge is normally included in the bill, but it is still usual to round up the amount you pay, though no more than 5 per cent. For cloakrooms, where a charge is not made, small change is an appropriate tip. Taxi drivers expect a 10 per cent tip.

TOILETS

Male and female facilities are indicated by a symbol or by the words *Herren* (Gentlemen) and *Damen* (Ladies). Always have small coins ready in case the door has a coin slot.

TOURIST INFORMATION

The German National Tourist Board (GNTB) – Deutsche Zentrale für Tourismus e.V. (DZT) – can give you information on when to go, where to stay and what to see in Germany. The headquarters is located at: Beethovenstrasse 69, 60325 Frankfurt-am-Main; www.germany.travel. The GNTB also maintains offices in many countries throughout the world:

Australia: GPO Box 1461, Sydney, NSW 2001, tel: 02 8296 0488

Canada: 2 Bloor Street West, Suite 2601, Toronto, ON M4W 3E2, tel: 416 935 1896

UK: PO Box 2695, London W1A 3TN, tel: 020 7317 0908

US: 122 East 42nd Street, 20th Floor, Suite 2000, New York, NY 10168-0072, tel: 212 661 7200

Once in the country, your first port of call should be the local tourist information centre, to be found in every city and in most towns. Many will book rooms and sell tickets for events.

Berlin: Pariser Platz, südliches Torhaus, 10117 Berlin, tel: 030 25 00 23 33; www.visitberlin.de

Munich: Sendlinger Strasse 1, 80331 München, tel: 089 2339 6500; www.muenchen.de

Dresden: Prager Strasse 2b, 01067 Dresden, tel: 0351 501 501; www.dresden.de

Cologne: Kardinal-Höffner-Platz 1, 50667 Köln, tel: 0221 346 430; www.koelntourismus.de

TRANSPORT

Air. Major cities are connected by domestic flights, many of them operated by the national airline, Lufthansa (tel: 01805 805 805; www.lufthansa.com).

Rail. DB (Deutsche Bahn, tel: 01805 996 633; www.bahn.de) trains are generally very comfortable and reliable, and the rail network is comprehensive. A small number of lines are run by private operators. Types of train include: ICE (Intercity-Express), a state-of-the-art train running at speeds of up to 330kmh (205mph); IC (Inter-City), only marginally less up-to-the-minute; RE (Regional-Express), modern trains filling in the gaps between ICE and IC services; and RB (RegionalBahn), trains handling local services.

Standard fares are not cheap, but there are many concessions and special tickets, among them the InterRail Germany Pass giving unlimited travel for any 3, 4, 6 or 8 days in any one month. A BahnCard giving substantial discounts on normal fares is really only useful for people travelling frequently in Germany.

Bus. Long-distance bus services are becoming popular in Germany and there are now many companies offering a clean, efficient service both nationally and internationally. The biggest operator is Flixbus (www.flixbus.de). Tickets can be bought online from ticketing sites, such as www.busliniensuche.de, or from travel agents, bus stations or the driver.

Ferries and riverboats. Ferries are the usual way of getting to the islands off the North Sea and Baltic coasts. Ferries also operate at places along the Rhine, Elbe and other rivers where there are no bridges. A trip on a white steamer along one of the main rivers is an essential component of a holiday in Germany, particularly on the middle Rhine (services operated by Köln-Düsseldorfer Deutsche Rheinschiffahrt; www.k-d.com), Mosel, lower Neckar and Elbe around Dresden (services operated by Sächsische Dampfschiffahrt; www.saechsische-dampfschiffahrt.de).

City transport. Larger cities have integrated transport systems based on trams, S-Bahn (suburban railway), buses and, in the case of Berlin, Frankfurt, Hamburg and Munich, underground railways (U-Bahn). Trams *(Strassenbahn)* often run underground in city centres. Tickets are normally interchangeable between the different modes. Day, three-day and weekly passes are available, and in some cities there are 'Welcome Cards', which give free or reduced-price entry to a range of attractions as well as unrestricted travel. Underground stations are identified by a white U on a blue background, S-Bahn stations by an S on a green background, bus and tram stops by a green H on a yellow background. After purchasing your ticket, validate it by cancelling it in one of the machines provided, either at the stop or on board the vehicle.

Where is the nearest bus/tram stop? **Wo ist die nächste Bus-/Strassenbahn-Haltestelle?**
I want a ticket to... **Ich will eine Fahrkarte nach...**
single/return **einfache Fahrt/Rückfahrkarte**

V

VISAS AND ENTRY REQUIREMENTS

Visitors from EU countries need an identity card or passport to enter Germany. Citizens of other countries, including the US, Canada, Australia and New Zealand, must have a valid passport. Nationals of other countries that do not have a reciprocal agreement with Germany need a visa. Regulations can change, so always check before you travel. EU nationals may import duty-free goods for personal use. There is no limit on the amount of foreign currency that may be brought in and out of the country.

W

WEBSITES AND INTERNET CAFÉS

Internet cafés abound in major German cities, and an increasing number of hotels provide internet facilities.

All German towns have a website, often with an English version, on the pattern of www.stuttgart.de, with quick access to the kind of information useful in planning a visit. Other websites include:

www.germany.travel German National Tourist Board.

www.bed-and-breakfast.de Lists and categorises B&B establishments throughout Germany.

www.hotelguide.de Lists thousands of German hotels.

www.dertour.de Travel information and booking service of the long-established German national travel agency, Der Tour.

Y

YOUTH HOSTELS

Germany's more than 500 youth hostels are listed on the website of the Deutsche Jugendherberge (German Association of Youth Hostels; www.djh.de); you can also call them at tel: 0711 166860. Book in advance in summer and at weekends. Youth hostels charge around €15 per person.

RECOMMENDED HOTELS

The following hotels in towns, cities and regions throughout Germany are listed under the major headings used in the Where to Go section. They include a number of modest but attractive establishments, as well as conventional luxury hotels. Advance booking is recommended, especially in summer. In cities such as Hanover, Cologne and Hamburg which have a programme of trade fairs, prices can double when a fair is in progress and accommodation will be difficult to find. In city or resort hotels special deals are often available at weekends.

As a basic guide to prices for a double room with breakfast we have used the following symbols:

€€€€	over 300 euros
€€€	200–300 euros
€€	100–200 euros
€	below 100 euros

BERLIN AND POTSDAM

Berlin

Adlon Kempinski €€€€ *Unter den Linden 77, tel: 030 22610*, www.kempinski.com. The location of this large, luxury hotel, right by the Brandenburg Gate, could hardly be bettered, nor could the hotel's standards of service, facilities and comfort. There's a pool, sauna and gym, and some of the suites have their own fitness rooms and sauna.

Art Nouveau €€€ *Leibnizstrasse 59, tel: 030 327 7440*, www.hotelartnouveau.de. Excellent location just off Kurfürstendamm for this well-run small establishment on the fourth floor of a stately century-old town house. Attractive modern bedrooms, some furnished with antiques. Across the street is *Leibniz* Klause, a restaurant famous for traditional German food.

Arte Luise Kunsthotel €€€ *Luisenstrasse 19, tel: 030 284 480*, www.luise-berlin.com. Centrally located near the Kanzleramt, one of Berlin's most extravagant art hotels has public spaces and 50 bedrooms graced by artworks, fittings and interior design by avant-garde designers.

Augustinenhof €€ *Auguststrasse 82, tel: 030 308 860*, www.hotel-augustinenhof.de. Once a Christian hospice, this attractive and comfortable establishment near Hackescher Markt is expertly run by the Berlin city mission. Equipped with a spa, sauna and tanning bed.

Honigmond Garden €€ *Invalidenstrasse 122, tel: 030 2844 5577*, www.honigmond-berlin.de. The restful garden of the hotel's name emphasises the quiet nature of an intimate little hotel with a sense of style in the old Scheunenviertiel district. Close to the Central Railway Station (Hauptbahnhof).

Ku'Damm 101 € *Kurfürstendamm 101, tel: 030 520 0550*, www.kudamm101.com. This 4-star hotel features modern Bauhaus-inspired design and spacious rooms. It's in a convenient location close to the main shopping boulevard and the central railway station. You can rent bikes in front of the hotel.

The Mandala €€€€ *Potsdamer Strasse 3, tel: 030 5900 50000*, www.the-mandala.de. Lavishly equipped designer hotel at Potsdamer Platz with impeccable service and an emphasis on wellness and relaxation.

Q! €€€ *Knesebeckstrasse 67, tel: 030 810 0660*, www.hotel-q.com. This trendy, medium-sized Charlottenburg establishment boasts lavish facilities, including an oriental-style wellness area.

Potsdam

Am Luisenplatz €€–€€€ *Luisenplatz 5, tel: 0331 971 900*, www.hotel-luisenplatz.de. In a convenient location between the centre of Potsdam and the park of Schloss Sanssouci, with a great view of the Brandenburg Gate, this elegant town hotel offers classically comfortable accommodation.

Schiffspension Luise € *Berliner Strasse 58, tel: 0331 24 02 22*, www.schiffspension.de. If you want somewhere unusual to stay, try this barge permanently anchored on the Havela river. Head to the main deck for views of Babelsberg Castle and Park.

Spreewald

Schloss Lübbenau €€–€€€ *Schlossbezirk 6, Lübbenau, tel: 03542 8730*, www.schlossluebbenau.de. With its comfortable rooms furnished in traditional style, this restored country seat makes an excellent base for exploring the delights of the watery countryside all around.

HAMBURG AND THE NORTH

Baltic Coast

Elisabeth von Eicken €–€€ *Dorfstrasse 39, Ostseebad Ahrenshoop, tel: 038220 67970*, www.elisabeth-voneicken.de. On the sandy Fischland peninsula, Ahrenshoop still retains the atmosphere of an early 20th-century artists' colony, nowhere more so than in this six-room Art Nouveau villa adorned with artworks.

Strandhotel Ostseeblick €€–€€€ *Kulmstrasse 28, Heringsdorf, tel: 038378 540*, www.strandhotel-ostseeblick.de. In the resort of Usedom Island, the award-winning family-run 'Seaview' Hotel lives up to its name, with many of its rooms enjoying Baltic vistas.

Vier Jahreszeiten Binz €€€ *Zeppelinstrasse 8, Binz, tel: 038393 500*, www.vier-jahreszeiten.eu. Built in traditional style, this luxury hotel in the heart of Rügen Island's premier resort offers every comfort and a wide range of facilities. It's close to the promenade and pier.

Bremen

Radisson Blu Hotel €€€€ *Böttcherstrasse 2, tel: 0421 36 960*, www.radissonblu.com. Large hotel with all the usual Radisson amenities plus a city-centre location on the architecturally distinguished Böttcherstrasse.

Hamburg

Gastwerk €€€ *Beim Alten Gaswerk 3, tel: 040 890 620*, www.gastwerk. com. A designer hotel that's a successful combination of old architecture and contemporary style, in the suburb of Bahrenfeld, 4km (2.5 miles) from the city centre.

Relexa Hotel Bellevue €€ *An der Alster 14, tel: 040 284 440*, www.relexa-hotels.de. This small and immaculately run establishment on the banks of the Alster prides itself on its service and its attractive, individually furnished rooms.

Vier Jahreszeiten €€€€ *Neuer Jungfernstieg 9–14, tel: 040 34 940*, www.hvj.de. Overlooking the Binnenalster lake, the 'Four Seasons' is a grand hotel with all the amenities you would expect. The dining is among the best in town.

Lübeck

Klassik Altstadt Hotel €€ *Fischergrube 52, tel: 0451 702 980*, www. klassik-altstadt-hotel.de. Small, family-run hotel in a fine old town mansion in a quiet location in the heart of the Hanseatic town. Attractive, comfortable rooms, themed to reflect prominent Lübeck personalities. Restaurant.

Mecklenburg Lake District

Seehotel Ecktannen €€ *Fontanestrasse 51, Waren, tel: 03991 6290*, www.ecktannen.de. Idyllically located and convenient for all the recreational activities available on the water and in the surrounding area, this pleasant small hotel offers attractive, inexpensive accommodation.

Rostock/Warnemünde

Hotel Sonne €€–€€€ *Neuer Markt 2, Rostock, tel: 0381 49 730*, www. steigenberger.com. This stylish establishment benefits from a central location on Rostock's market square and offers an excellent range of facilities.

Wilhelmshöhe €–€€ *Waldweg 1, Diedrichshagen, tel: 0381 548 280*, www. ostseehotel-wilhelmshoehe.de. Friendly, small hotel amid lovely natural surroundings on the coast to the west of Warnemünde. Ask for a room with a balcony facing the Baltic.

DRESDEN AND THE TWO SAXONYS
Dresden

Kempinski Hotel Taschenberg Palais €€€€ *Taschenberg 3, tel: 0351 49 120*, www.kempinski.com. Sumptuous palace in the very heart of Dresden, offering its guests every possible comfort and convenience.

Villa Weltemühle €€€ *Merbitzer Strasse 53, Dresden-Briesnitz, tel: 0351 42 550*, www.hotel-weltemuehle.com. This establishment in Dresden's western suburb of Briesnitz has a gourmet restaurant complementing its attractive rooms and other lavish facilities.

Schloss Eckberg €€€ *Bautzner Strasse 134, Dresden-Loschwitz, tel: 0351 80 990*, www.schloss-eckberg.de. Set in parkland, this romantic Gothic Revival castle has varied styles of accommodation in tastefully furnished, comfortable rooms.

Leipzig

Hotel Fürstenhof €€€€ *Tröndlinring 8, tel: 0341 1400*, www.hotel fuerstenhofleipzig.com. Leipzig's centrally located, leading hotel is in a renovated 18th-century palace and offers the highest standards of service, facilities and comfort.

Victor's Residenz-Hotel €€–€€€ *Georgiring 13, tel: 0341 68 660*, www. victors.de. Opposite Leipzig's famous railway terminus, this comfortable establishment makes an excellent base for exploring the centre and the Old Town.

Saxon Switzerland

Romantik Hotel Tuchmacher €€–€€€ *Peterstrasse 8, Görlitz, tel: 03581 47 310*, www.tuchmacher.de. Three restored Renaissance buildings have been amalgamated to form this handsome hotel in the heart of the Old Town. The restaurant serves exquisite Silesian specialities.

WEIMAR AND THURINGIA
Eisenach

Hotel auf der Wartburg €€€€ *Auf der Wartburg 2, tel: 03691 7970*, www.wartburghotel.de. Beneath the Wartburg Castle, this traditional establishment offers supreme comfort as well as vistas over the Thuringian Forest. First-class restaurant.

Gotha

Landhaus Hotel Romantik € *Salzgitterstrasse 76, tel: 03621 36 490*, www.landhaus-hotel-romantik.de. A small and attractive family-run establishment on the eastern outskirts of the old ducal capital, with a courtyard terrace and a charming garden.

Weimar

Hotel Elephant €€€€ *Markt 19, tel: 03643 8020*, www.hotelelephant weimar.com. Weimar's most famous place to stay, in operation since 1696. Dine in the renowned Anna Amalia gourmet restaurant or, more affordably, in the rustic cellar.

HANOVER AND THE HARZ
Goslar

Das Brusttuch €€ *Hoher Weg 1, tel: 05321 34 600*, www.brusttuch.de. This 500-year-old mansion is richly ornamented and is located on the

town's market square. An intimate small hotel with a swimming pool and spa, it is a good starting point for hikes in the Harz mountains.

Hameln

Christinenhof €–€€ *Alte Marktstrasse 18, tel: 05151 95080*, https://christinenhof.de. Hameln's traditional style at its best is on show in a surprisingly contemporary old lodging in the heart of town that manages to fit in a swimming pool and modest wellness options.

Hanover

Kastens Hotel Luisenhof €€€€ *Luisenstrasse 1–3, tel: 0511 30 440*, www.kastens-luisenhof.de. Centrally located between Hanover's opera house and the main railway station, this historic hotel is a city institution, offering its guests the best in comfort and range of facilities. Gourmet restaurant.

Quedlinburg

Hotel Theophano €€ *Markt 13–14, tel: 03946 96 300*, www.hoteltheophano.de. Charming establishment consisting of three linked historic buildings on Quedlinburg's main square. Atmospheric cellar restaurant.

Wernigerode

Gothisches Haus €–€€€ *Marktplatz 2, tel: 03943 6750*, www.travelcharme.com/gothisches-haus. Historic 15th-century edifice on Wernigerode's marketplace offers every comfort, as well as traditional atmosphere. Facilities include extensive 'wellness' area. Choice of restaurants.

COLOGNE, THE RUHR AND RHINE
Cologne

Excelsior Hotel Ernst €€€€ *Trankgasse 1–5, Domplatz, tel: 0221 2701*, www.excelsiorhotelernst.com. An oasis of tranquillity, this 150-year-old establishment is located right opposite the cathedral. Luxurious rooms are a tasteful blend of modernity and tradition. Gourmet restaurant.

Das Kleine Stapelhäuschen €€ *Fischmarkt 1–3, tel: 0221 272 7777*, www.kleines-stapelhaeuschen.de. This narrow-fronted old edifice stands in Cologne's Altstadt right by the River Rhine. Characterful, highly individual rooms and a restaurant serving hearty food.

Düsseldorf

Orangerie €€–€€€ *Bäckergasse 1, tel: 0211 866 800*, www.hotel-orangerie-mcs.de. In a quiet part of the Altstadt free of through-traffic, this hotel in an attractive neoclassical building offers stylish contemporary rooms.

Münster

Hof zur Linde €€–€€€€ *Handorfer Werseufer 1, Münster-Handorf, tel: 0251 32 750*, www.hof-zur-linde.de. Just beyond the city limits and easily accessible from the Autobahn, this establishment's origins go back to the 17th century. The rustic hideaway has a pleasant riverbank location and a choice of comfortable, characterful rooms and suites.

The Rhine

Bellevue Rheinhotel €€–€€€ *Rheinallee 41, Boppard, tel: 06742 1020*, www.bellevue-boppard.de. On the riverside promenade of one of the Rhine gorge's most attractive towns, this stately establishment is impeccably run.

Speyer

Domhof €€ *Bauhof 3, tel: 06232 13290*, www.domhof.de. Tucked virtually into the shadow of Speyer's great cathedral, this hotel-restaurant with its own house brewery has modern little rooms set in an old-world ambiance.

SOUTHWEST TO THE BLACK FOREST
Baden-Baden

Hotel am Markt € *Marktplatz 18, tel: 07221 27 040*, www.hotel-am-markt-baden.de. Family-run small hotel in a quiet location in Baden-Baden's Altstadt, with straightforward but elegant rooms.

Frankfurt

Liebig-Hotel €€€ *Liebigstrasse 45, tel: 069 215 02*, www.hotelliebig.de. Small hotel in an exclusive residential district in Frankfurt's west end, offering a choice between simply furnished and more elaborately decorated rooms at reasonable rates.

Steigenberger Frankfurter Hof €€€€ *Am Kaiserplatz 1, tel: 069 21 502*, www.steigenberger.com. The listed Frankfurter Hof is a showcase for the prestigious Steigenberger hotel group. Expensive, but everything a grand hotel should be. Modern spa and panoramic views.

Freiburg

Markgräfler Hof €€–€€€ *Gerberau 22, tel: 0761 32 540*, www.markgraeflerhof-freiburg.de. Exquisite hotel in a renovated neoclassical palace in Freiburg's 'Little Venice'. Comfortable, country-style rooms, wine bar and one of Freiburg's best restaurants.

Heidelberg

Deidesheimer Hof €€–€€€ *Marktplatz 1, Deidesheim, tel: 06326 96 870*, www.deidesheimerhof.de. Tastefully furnished rooms in a historic hostelry that also offers superb cuisine.

Zum Ritter St Georg €€€ *Hauptstrasse 178, tel: 06221 705 050*, www.hotel-ritter-heidelberg.com. Stay in style on Heidelberg's main street, in one of the city's loveliest town mansions, dating from the late 16th century. The quieter rooms are in the modern extension to the rear.

Lake Constance

Hotel Löwen €–€€ *Marktplatz 2*, Meersburg am Bodensee, *tel: 07532 43 040*, www.hotel-loewen-meersburg.de. Five-hundred-year-old inn on the market square in the upper part of this lakeside town, with lots of atmosphere and attractive, comfortable rooms.

Stuttgart

Ochsen €€ *Ulmer Strasse 323, Stuttgart-Wangen, tel: 0711 407 0500,* www.ochsen-online.de. Family-run, timber-framed 18th-century inn close to the River Neckar and 15 minutes by public transport to the city centre. Stylish bedrooms, some with Jacuzzi.

MUNICH AND THE SOUTH

Bavarian Alps

Gasthof Fraundorfer €–€€ *Ludwigstrasse 24, Garmisch-Partenkirchen, tel: 08821 9270*, www.gasthof-fraundorfer.de. Pleasantly rustic rooms in a charming old inn with typical Bavarian paintings. Folklore evenings in the equally rustic restaurant.

Vier Jahreszeiten €–€€ *Maximilianstrasse 20, Berchtesgaden, tel: 08652 9520*, www.hotel-vierjahreszeiten-berchtesgaden.de. Central hotel with attractive and comfortable panelled rooms, some with superb Alpine views. Breakfast terrace and indoor pool.

Munich

Bayerischer Hof €€€€ *Promenadeplatz 2–6, tel: 089 21 200*, www.bay-erischerhof.de. Family-run for over a century, this grand hotel is a city institution. Its restaurant Atelier with Silent Garden has three Michelin stars and there are concerts in the piano bar on Fridays.

Gästehaus Englischer Garten €€–€€€ *Liebergesellstrasse 8, tel: 089 383 9410*, www.hotelenglischergarten.de. Charming small establishment in a converted watermill right by Munich's largest park, the Englischer Garten. Book well in advance.

Kempinski Vier Jahreszeiten €€€€ *Maximilianstrasse 17, tel: 089 21 250*, www.kempinski.com. Munich's 'other' grand hotel, the haunt of celebrities since 1858, offering every amenity in the heart of the city.

NUREMBERG AND NORTHERN BAVARIA
Bamberg

St Nepomuk €€–€€€€ *Obere Mühlbrücke 9, tel: 0951 98 420*, www.hotel-nepomuk.de. Converted mill and charming old annexes offer individually designed and furnished rooms of great comfort.

Nuremberg

Agneshof €€–€€€ *Agnesgasse 10, tel: 0911 214 440*, www.agneshof-nuernberg.de. Centrally located in a side street, this medium-sized establishment offers attractive rooms – some with a view of the castle – and a courtyard garden.

Regensburg

Bischofshof €€€ *Krauterermarkt 3, tel: 0941 58 460*, www.hotel-bischofshof.de. Former bishop's palace in the heart of Regensburg. Quiet, individually furnished rooms.

Rothenburg Ob Der Tauber

Romantik Hotel Markusturm €€–€€€ *Rödergasse 1, tel: 09861 94 280*, www.markusturm.de. Intimate establishment in a building dating from the 13th century, next to a beautiful medieval gateway. Charming, individually furnished rooms.

INDEX

INSIGHT ⊙ GUIDES POCKET GUIDE

GERMANY

First Edition 2018

Editor: Ros Walford
Author: Mike Ivory, George McDonald
Head of DTP and Pre-Press: Rebeka Davies
Picture Editor: Tom Smyth
Cartography Update: Carte
Update Production: Apa Digital
Photography Credits: 123RF 74, 133;
4Corners Images 1; Chris Coe/Apa
Publications 110; Getty Images 5TC, 23, 24,
28, 91; Glyn Genin/Apa Publications 7R, 52,
63, 67, 68, 72, 85, 86, 147, 150; iStock 4MC,
4ML, 4TL, 5T, 5MC, 5M, 6R, 7, 11, 12, 15, 17,
26, 31, 33, 35, 39, 44, 46, 48, 51, 56, 59, 61, 64,
71, 77, 79, 80, 83, 89, 92, 95, 96, 99, 101, 103,
105, 106, 108, 111, 116, 118, 120, 123, 125,
126, 129, 130, 135, 136, 138, 145; Jon Santa
Cruz/Apa Publications 5MC, 6L, 37, 41, 43,
143, 149; Public domain 5M, 18, 20, 113;
Shutterstock 4TC, 55; Tom Smyth 115
Cover Picture: Shutterstock

Distribution
UK, Ireland and Europe: Apa Publications
(UK) Ltd; sales@insightguides.com
United States and Canada: Ingram
Publisher Services; ips@ingramcontent.com
Australia and New Zealand: Woodslane;
info@woodslane.com.au
Southeast Asia: Apa Publications (SN) Pte;
singaporeoffice@insightguides.com
Worldwide: Apa Publications (UK) Ltd;
sales@insightguides.com

**Special Sales, Content Licensing
and CoPublishing**
Insight Guides can be purchased in bulk
quantities at discounted prices. We can
create special editions, personalised jackets
and corporate imprints tailored to your
needs. sales@insightguides.com;
www.insightguides.biz

All Rights Reserved
© 2018 Apa Digital (CH) AG and
Apa Publications (UK) Ltd
Printed in China by CTPS

No part of this book may be reproduced,
stored in a retrieval system or transmitted in
any form or means electronic, mechanical,
photocopying, recording or otherwise, without
prior written permission from Apa Publications.

Contact us
Every effort has been made to provide accurate
information in this publication, but changes are
inevitable. The publisher cannot be responsible
for any resulting loss, inconvenience or injury.
We would appreciate it if readers would call our
attention to any errors or outdated information.
We also welcome your suggestions; please
contact us at: hello@insightguides.com
www.insightguides.com